COMPUTING

MORALITY

0100011000011111110010011001111101111011001100000111010011011100001111111100011000000110010011
0011000010010001100110011001111111111000110011011000000011010010000000011111111111110010100110010
1011010000011001011110110000111010010100000000101101111101111000011001100110111111111011000011
10011110010111100011110001011011000111101100001001000110001111100100100011011011100111100100011

COMPUTING MORALITY

0100011000011111110010011001111101111011001100000111010011011100001111111100011000000110010011
0011000010010001100110011001111111111000110011011000000011010010000000011111111111110010100110010
1011010000011001011110110000111010010100000000101101111101111000011001100110111111111011000011
10011110010111100011110001011011000111101100001001000110001111100100100011011011100111100100011

A COMPUTER SCIENTIST'S APPROACH TO
ETHICS AND ECONOMICS

BENJAMIN CHANG

Computing Morality:
A Computer Scientist's Approach to Ethics and Economics

For information about this title or to order other books
and/or electronic media, contact the publisher:

Benjamin Chang
benjamin.chang.cmu@gmail.com

ISBNs:
978-1-7361807-0-9 (print)
978-1-7361807-1-6 (eBook)

Printed in the United States of America

Cover and Interior design: 1106 Design

For Mom, Dad, Jeffrey, Buddy, and Kevin

Contents

Foreword

THE WORLD IS BECOMING MORE COMPLEX. The level of expertise required to succeed sometimes takes, it seems, an entire lifetime to master. There are even those who propose that life and society have become so complicated that we should rely on experts to tell us how to live our lives, organize our societies, and, most terrifyingly of all, tell us what is right or wrong.

In our modern political scene, we have heard statements from those "experts" and those in power numerous times:

Your right to free speech shouldn't infringe on others' rights not to hear your rude and hateful language.

How can everyone be free if the poor are never truly free? Your right to freedom is not more important than a poor person's right to provide for himself.

Have you ever been homeless? It is immoral to have people homeless while others can afford ten mansions.

There are people today who constantly hear language like this and know deep down that there is something fundamentally wrong with the above statements. However, they have trouble explaining why.

Great philosophers and economists have already written many works that show why values that focus on liberty lead to better lives for everyone. However, many of their works are inaccessible to young people. It is a constant uphill battle to get younger people to understand the importance of the liberties we take for granted today. The goal of this book is to explain systematically and precisely to people why the above statements are morally wrong or inconsistent. To do so requires one to have a basic but broad and consistent ethical, economic, and political model of how the world works. This book takes a multidisciplinary approach to looking at the world, relying heavily on math, natural sciences, formal logic, and computer science. Surprisingly, I regularly use concepts that I learned studying computer science at Carnegie Mellon to argue best for why a free society is a just society. Who would have known that concepts such as Kurt Gödel's Incompleteness Theorems, the Principle of Explosion, or Proofs by Contradiction would apply to politics and ethics?

The first section of the book will construct a morally consistent ethical system that values free trade and liberty; I will use powerful concepts borrowed from logic and computer science. Then, I'll show why many attempts at altering that framework are not logically and ethically consistent, leading to dangerous contradictions. The second section will use examples from mathematics to construct a simple but all-encompassing model for how the world works from an economic standpoint. I'll briefly explain important concepts that many socialists and conservatives alike fail to grasp. I hope to show how a free-market system is one that best reflects and overcomes the problems of nature. The last section will briefly tie the two concepts together to explain why we have the political system we have today.

WHY DO WE NEED MODELS?

Politics is as divisive as ever. Every day, pundits on both sides of the aisle stoop lower and lower to cram their ideas and agendas down someone's throat. Most discussions involve half-truths and cherry-picked data to selectively highlight the efficacy of certain policies. Very little is a discussion on the fundamentals of ethics.

For example, take the following question, asked in the first 2016 Presidential debate between Donald Trump and Hillary Clinton: Why are you a better choice than your opponent to create the kinds of jobs that will put more money into the pockets of American workers?

Consider this excerpt from Trump's reply: "Our jobs are fleeing the country. They're going to Mexico. They're going to many other countries. . . . So, we're losing our good jobs, so many of them. . . . So, Ford is leaving. You see that—their small-car division leaving. Thousands of jobs leaving Michigan, leaving Ohio. They're all leaving. And we can't allow it to happen anymore. . . . We have to stop them from leaving."

While, on the surface, it seems great that the President is advocating for the well-being of the average American, the moral implications of his proposed actions are questionable: Can the government prevent a company from moving operations overseas and force them to stay inside the country? If so, is that any different, in principle, than forcing an individual who wants to work overseas to stay within the United States? Does any amount of benefit received by keeping jobs within the U.S. justify forceful measures to control where people are allowed to work?

In another example, consider an excerpt from Clinton's response: "I want us to invest in your future. That means jobs in infrastructure, in advanced manufacturing, innovation and technology, clean, renewable energy, and small business. . . . [Independent experts] have looked at my plans and they've said, 'We will have 10 million more new jobs, because we will be making investments where we can grow the economy.'"

How do "independent experts" estimate the number of jobs to be created by policy? Are 10 million well-paying jobs enough of a benefit to justify forceful investment into areas that an individual would not have done otherwise? Can a government force someone to invest his or her money into an area it deems to be "important"? If so, how many jobs created are enough to justify such an investment of taxpayers' dollars? Is one job enough or five million jobs too few? In principle, is there any difference between forceful investment by the government in green energy than in adult films or in modern dance?

I've heard similar debates among people talking about why their policies are most effective, haphazardly presenting misleading data, personal anecdotes, and a myriad of sketchy studies. Such discourse rarely, if ever, changes any minds. Statistics are questioned, data are scrutinized, and no matter how accurate they may be, there will always be some data point or anecdote thrown back to refute almost any assertion. Usually, upon closer investigation, one person's data is misleading or simply wrong.

However, many times you don't have your opponent's data source handy, and you have to go back and research your opponent's claims to come up with a rebuttal. Debates end up being a slugfest of random data points, with debaters artfully dodging questions whenever they can. To decide who is the "winner" of these debates, people vote. We see articles like CNBC's "Who Won the Final 2016 Debate?" which states that "an instant poll from CNN/ORC showed Clinton with a broad advantage."

Truth and morals cannot be decided by a popular vote. If most of the nation votes that stealing should be legal, does any reasonable person believe that such an action is moral and right? Debates focus too much on the results of public policy, which can be extremely difficult to measure. Many advocates of liberty and free markets try to argue their case by using data to show that, in an overwhelming majority of cases, free trade leads to a better standard of life, and there certainly is a ton of data supporting this. Conservative commentator Ben Shapiro loves to say that "Facts don't care about your feelings" and heavily uses data and evidence from studies to prove his points. However, data are messy and can always be skewed to show something different.

When bogged down by details and numbers, people usually can't see the forest for the trees. Instead of trying to figure out if an action is right or wrong, they try to find examples of why doing something is *effective*, which can lead to some dangerous conclusions. It was common practice to educate Roman slaves, who often had jobs such as tutoring, accounting, and in medicine—in a world in which the total literacy rate was less than 5-20%.[1,2] Even if there is data to show that systematic slavery increases the education and literacy rate of its slaves, in practice, it is unlikely that anyone will pitch encouraging systematic slavery as a policy.

This is because deep inside, we know slavery doesn't *feel* right. In other words, we can confidently say that slavery is *wrong*. Our feelings—which Mr. Shapiro dismisses—are crucial in deciding what is right and what is wrong. However, without a basic moral model, we don't know *why* it is morally wrong. This is why feelings alone will not suffice. Every time we are met with a new situation, we can't let something as subjective as feelings guide our actions—that can result in disaster. A better term for "feelings" is "values," and the question we should be asking ourselves is, "What basic values do we have that lead us to the conclusion that slavery is wrong, and why do we have such values?" To answer these questions, we need to first have a moral framework constructed from our most basic values.

Developing a mental model allows people to identify key values. If someone fundamentally feels that human life has no value, there is no point in debating with that person over why a policy that legalizes murder and pillaging would be detrimental for society. At the same time, it also tells us that, if someone, at the most basic level, has vastly different and potentially harmful values, people who believe that human life is sacred should do everything in their power to protect themselves and their values.

Mental models are also crucial for tying important ideas together. A moral framework does not exist in a vacuum. We need to understand that we have certain morals due to the constraints of the world, which we must examine through a natural scientist's lens. For example, would we really think stealing is wrong if people had the magical ability to wish their favorite things from a genie in a bottle? Therefore, a moral framework is not enough. We also need to have a basic understanding of how the world works, which means we need to have a basic economic model. Finally, we need to know how best to execute our moral and economic framework, which leads us very briefly into the realm of politics.

If we have two people who agree on basic values but disagree on a certain policy or action, then we have a framework for debate. The goal of the debate is to show that one person's moral system *contradicts* the very basic values he or she believes in. For example, if you and another person both abhor forced labor, you both believe that it is morally wrong to compel someone to work without wages. But, let's say that the other person is an advocate of total income redistribution due to some random statistic. Then your job is to show that any policy that redistributes income is tantamount to taking away one's labor to give to another by force. In other words, it is a policy that he or she may claim to be effective but is morally inconsistent with that person's most basic values. This person needs to a) renounce such a policy or b) admit that he or she doesn't really believe that it is morally wrong to compel someone to work.

STRUCTURE OF ARGUMENT

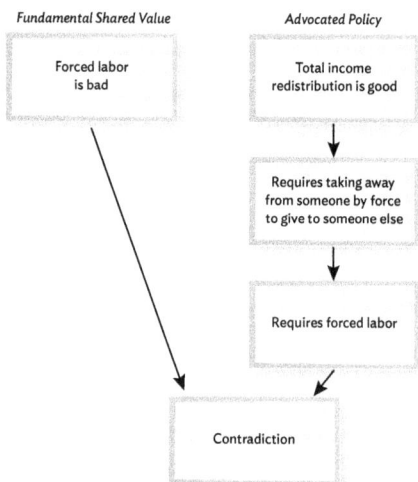

Fundamental Shared Value

Forced labor is bad

Advocated Policy

Total income redistribution is good

Requires taking away from someone by force to give to someone else

Requires forced labor

Contradiction

WHY COMPUTER SCIENCE?

To have any sort of meaningful debate, people must have shared values. For example, the most successful and common shared values are "Life is good" and "People should not kill other people." Then, using those agreed-upon values and tools we borrow from the realm of mathematics, logic, and computer science, we can proceed to debate whether certain actions agree with those shared values in an airtight fashion. The goal of debate is to show that a set of actions taken or proposed by the other side contradicts the very values they said to have believed in.

Today, people use the word "logical" too liberally. In most instances, there is no formal logical step taken when this word is thrown around, and it's usually followed by some non sequitur. When we discuss logic from a mathematician's or computer scientist's lens, we mean something very rigorous. We mean the same logic that computers use every single day to figure out what angle a wing flap on a 160-ton Boeing jet should be and the same logic that mathematicians at Bletchley Park used to crack the Enigma code, which saved millions of lives. In this system, we must prove precisely one logical statement after another. For example:

Provided we have two statements that both parties agree upon, such as

1. All men are mortal.
2. Socrates is a man.

Then, both sides must agree that, therefore, Socrates is mortal.

To deny the above is to deny truth. If a system of morals can be shown to be illogical or contradictory, we can go on to show that such a system of morals cannot hold.

Logic is the perfect means for thinking about ethics. The computers we rely on every day use logic gates and bits. No one questions the output of properly written computer code and formally constructed logical statements. In the modern world, people entrust their lives to it. Computers think only in binary states of 0s and 1s. Life and nature, too, when boiled down to their simplest, are binary. A human being is either living or dead, with nothing in between. One action cannot be both right and wrong at the same time. One set of actions allows people to thrive and to live, and another leads to misery and death.

PART I

CREATING AN ETHICAL MENTAL MODEL FROM SCRATCH

Laying the Groundwork
Boring Computer Science Topics Made Fun

Definitions, Definitions, Definitions

Computer scientists and logicians are obsessed with definitions. Most proofs simply try to show that something meets the definition of another thing. To prove something true or false, we must define our terms as specifically as possible. Then, we must lean on these definitions. Consider the following example:

Show that the statement "6 is an even number" is true.

This proof essentially requires us to show that 6 meets the *definition* of an even number. The most obvious way to define an even number would be the following:

A number is even if it is divisible by 2.

However, we now need to define what "divisible" means, and we need to continue doing so until all non-common English terms are formally defined. You'll notice that, in legal documents, almost every other word starts with a capital letter. This is because those words are formally defined in an appendix of definitions. Definitions restrict the number of interpretations of a statement and allow us to make formal conclusions.

Now, we must define what "divisible" means:

A number "n" is divisible by a number "d" if "n" can be divided by "d" without a remainder.

Now, we need to define what a "remainder" is. I'll simply say that a remainder is whatever is left over after division. I'll refrain from defining what "divide" means, for it seems obvious, and I do not want to re-create mathematics and the English language from scratch. However, if you are interested in what a full, ground-up definition of "divides" is, visit https://proofwiki.org/wiki/Definition:Division

Now, we can prove that 6 is an even number:

By the definition of "divisible," since 6 is divided by 2 without a remainder, 6 is divisible by 2.

Therefore, *by the definition of* "even number,"
since 6 is divisible by 2, 6 is an even number.

Put more simply, all we did was establish a chain of definitions to show that 6 meets some specific criteria to be classified as an even number. Definitions are the fundamental building blocks of proofs.

Just as in financial and legal documents, from now on, I will capitalize terms that I associate with a very specific definition in mind. All instances of words that are yet to be defined will be in **boldface**. These terms will be defined as you read along.

COMPUTER SCIENCE TOPIC #2:

An Important Corollary—Language and References

Earlier, I had to make an important statement that I was not going to redefine every word in the English language. This is crucial, because, to have any meaningful definition, we must come to some level of agreement on what certain words mean. For example, even if every person on the planet defines even numbers the same way, someone could still very much dispute the statement "6 is an even number" if he disputes what the definition of "is" is. If both parties speak English but their interpretations of common English syntax and words are disputed, there can be no progress forward.

Language, when used correctly and precisely, is not ambiguous. That doesn't mean that there are no ambiguous statements. For example, the statement "This shirt is green" is a fairly straightforward one. However, this statement can be true to some and false for others. One might fairly say that the shirt is more of a bluish-turquoise color instead of pure green.

To correct for this flaw of ambiguous language, we simply need to agree upon references ahead of time. For objects and descriptions of actions that occur in nature, we have a reference that we can point to. If we agree ahead of time that green means rgb (0, 128, 0)—this is a computer's way of generating a specific color—then there is no ambiguity in determining whether the statement "This shirt is green" is true or false. As long as someone is precise with his language and fixes any potentially ambiguous language with a specific reference, there should be no problems with coming up with a mutually agreed-upon set of definitions that are *not* open to interpretation.

COMPUTER SCIENCE TOPIC #3:

Choosing Your Axioms for the Perfect Axiomatic System

Any mathematical or logical **System** starts off with **Axioms**.

A **System** is a set of rules that govern any possible behavior that allows someone to arrive at a conclusion or decision in an **Exhaustive** and **Deterministic** manner. **Exhaustive** means that the System needs to be able to handle *any* valid input that comes in. In other words, we can't have an input which our System does not know what to do with. **Deterministic** means that there is no randomness involved.

If the same input comes more than once into the System, the System will lead to the same output or conclusion it led to the first time that input was introduced.

For a real-life example:

Let's say we are building an English dictionary from scratch, and the System we choose to order words is alphabetical order.

This System is Deterministic because there is only one way to sort words alphabetically. If you give me a new word, I will always know the exact place to put it in my dictionary, and if you give it to me again tomorrow, I will put it in the same place. This System is also Exhaustive because, no matter the word that you show me (even non-words such as "qwerty"), I will be able to add it to my dictionary in the proper manner.

However, if I were building an English and Chinese dictionary, this System wouldn't work, because it wouldn't be Exhaustive. If I introduce the character "#" to be put into my dictionary, our System of alphabetical order grinds to a halt. Therefore, we would need to expand or change the System to allow it to meet the criteria set forth above.

Axioms are the Big Bang of logical Systems. They are statements we must assume to be true from the very start, since we can't prove something from nothing. The choice of Axioms generally meets the following criteria: Each Axiom is self-evident, the set of Axioms chosen does not allow someone to prove a **Contradiction** (which I will define more formally later on), the set of Axioms is finite, and the set of Axioms chosen should be as few as possible to allow us to prove as much as possible.

This is easy to understand. If our System chooses assumptions that seem false, leads to **Contradictions**, or requires a new rule for everything that it can't handle, it is generally a worthless System. Imagine if you had a school rule book that had to add a new rule for every single thing someone does. Imagine that it said, "No one should run in the hallways" *and* "Third-graders are allowed to run in the hallways." What a nightmare!

The richness and power of a System with well-chosen Axioms is astounding. Everything we do in arithmetic—from counting numbers to multiplication and division—can be described by the Zermelo-Fraenkel Set Theory with the Axiom of Choice, which has only *nine* Axioms! Axioms then allow us to prove truths that *must* follow from our assumptions, called **Theorems**.

COMPUTER SCIENCE TOPIC #4:

The Counter Example

Proving a general case is usually challenging. For example, if I had to prove that all swans were white, there are not many ways to go about doing it. I could show you ten white swans, but who's to say that the eleventh swan will be white? The simplest, but certainly not the easiest, way of doing so is to catch every swan on the planet and then show that all swans are, indeed, white. Or, we need to show it indirectly. For example, we could have a biologist slice up the swan genome and show that no mutation is possible for there to be a non-white swan.

Disproving something is shockingly easy. I would simply find one non-white swan and show it to you. The statement "All swans are white" is, therefore, false. This method of proof (or disproof) is called the **Counter Example**.

COMPUTER SCIENCE TOPIC #5:

The Principle of Explosion: Contradictions Are Bad

A **Contradiction** is a statement that is both true and false at the same time. Why are we so concerned about Contradictions? Computer scientists and logicians avoid Contradictions like the plague because, when any such Contradiction is proven in a logical system, *everything* is suddenly true, and *everything* is suddenly false, all at once! We call this the **Principle of Explosion**.

Let's assume that I am trying to prove that the statement "I am the best tennis player in the world" is true. In our System, we choose the following Contradictory Axioms:

1. Tennis is a fun sport
2. Tennis is not a fun sport

Now, I have all that's needed to prove that the statement "I am the best tennis player in the world" is true. We'll do it using the following method:

Since we have Axiom 1), we can show that

At least one of these statements is true:

    a. tennis is a fun sport (this is true because of Axiom 1)
    b. I am the best tennis player in the world

Now, using Axiom 2) and the above statement, we can show

At least one of these statements is true:

    a. ~~tennis is a fun sport~~ (this is not true because of Axiom 2)
    b. I am the best tennis player in the world

Therefore, we can deduce that statement b)—I am the best tennis player in the world—must be true since at least one of a) or b) must be true, and in this case, a) is not true, due to Axiom 2). Substitute that ridiculous claim b) with any arbitrary statement, and we have shown that anything can be proven to be true, and, very easily, that anything can be proven to be false.

COMPUTER SCIENCE TOPIC #6:

The Proof by Contradiction

The fact that we need to choose Axioms that don't lead to Contradictions is extremely important. Systems that don't lead to any Contradictions are called **Consistent**. The Consistency of a System is an extraordinarily powerful tool. It allows us to immediately conclude that, if a statement is true, the opposite of that statement is false. It also allows us to prove something by using a method called **Proof by Contradiction**. Proofs by Contradiction work like this: Assume the thing you are trying to prove is false. Proceed to prove that using that assumption leads to a Contradiction, in which something is both true and false at the same time. Therefore, your initial assumption cannot be false and, therefore, must be true.

We use Proofs by Contradiction every day without even knowing it. Consider the following example:

In the *Case of the Purloined Cookies*, Sherlock Holmes is trying to figure out whether his number-one suspect, Anna, was the one who stole the cookies from the top shelf. The top shelf is at a height of more than six feet, and there is nothing available to stand on that would enable someone shorter than six feet to reach the top shelf. With his measuring tape, he makes the following observations:

1. Anna is less than six feet tall
2. The person who stole the cookies must be six feet or taller.

It *seems obvious* that Anna could not have been the one who stole the cookies. However, the way to rigorously *prove* this fact is to use a Proof by Contradiction.

Let's assume that Anna stole the cookies. By observation 2), this means that Anna must be six feet or taller. However, we know from observation 1) that Anna is less than six feet tall. Therefore, we have shown that *if we assume Anna stole the cookies*, then Anna *must be* six feet or taller *and* she *must be* less than six feet tall. This is a Contradiction, since Anna cannot be both shorter than six feet and six feet or taller at the same the time. Therefore, our initial assumption that Anna stole the cookies must be false. This is how we formally rule out Anna as a suspect.

Proofs by Contradiction are incredibly powerful. Some of the greatest theoretical concepts in computer science, such as Alan Turing's proof of the existence of undecidable problems, are short Proofs by Contradiction.

COMPUTER SCIENCE TOPIC #7:

Gödel's Incompleteness Theorems

One important thing we need to consider is that we immediately concluded in our Proof by Contradiction example that Anna cannot be both shorter than six feet and six feet or taller at the same time. While this may seem obvious, we did not actually prove it. Why can't she be both taller than six feet and shorter than six feet at the same time? We just accept that this can't be and that, in nature, it is impossible for Contradictions to happen. In other words, we had to *assume* that the logical System that we and Sherlock Holmes use every day is Consistent and cannot have Contradictions. We have *made an assumption* about the truth of a statement—we have not *proven or disproven* the truth of that statement.

Why don't we try to prove that our logical framework is Consistent and free of Contradictions? German mathematician Kurt Gödel proved in 1931 that any formal System that is powerful enough to describe a Turing machine (or computer) will not be able to prove its own Consistency. In fact, he showed that a System is either **Inconsistent** or **Incomplete**. **Inconsistent** means that a System can prove a Contradiction. **Incomplete** means there are things that the System cannot prove and that, in this case, our current logical System cannot prove its own Consistency. This means there is a tradeoff between being Consistent (or right) and being able to prove everything!

Gödel's proof itself is also a Proof by Contradiction and is quite lengthy, but an important takeaway from this idea is that any complex System we assume to be Consistent will not be able to prove itself Consistent. Therefore, the best way to counter an Inconsistent moral System is to come up with specific examples that demonstrate that it is Inconsistent (i.e., a Counter Example). The burden of proof of the Inconsistency of any proposed moral System is, therefore, on those who disagree with it. However, one should try to challenge one's own moral system to test that it is, indeed, Consistent.

MORAL SYSTEMS ARE LOGICAL SYSTEMS

(e.g., **Computer Systems**)

We can see why moral Systems are the same as logical Systems.

- If a moral System is not constructed of finite assumptions, we can always introduce another rule into our system to make it okay. How useful can a System be if you can haphazardly add new rules to the System as you see fit?
- If a moral System does not allow us to deduce whether a certain action is right or wrong, we have a System that is, essentially, not Exhaustive. Of what use is a System if it grinds to a halt when situations that our System doesn't know how to handle arise all the time?
- If a moral system is not Deterministic, then it creates chaos. Of what use is a System that tells us that murder is evil today but is allowable the next day if nothing has changed?

- A System that governs nature cannot have Contradictions, because there are no Contradictions in nature itself. Someone cannot be dead and alive at the same time. Someone can't be in jail and not in jail at the same time. An action cannot be right and wrong at the same time. Moral truths are just as real as logical truths. If a moral System does Contradict itself, it is the worst of sins. Of what use is a System that says something is both good and evil? As we have shown from the Principle of Explosion, when there is a Contradiction in a moral System, *everything* is wrong, but, more dangerously, *everything* is right (like pillaging and murder).

- If moral Systems are not logical Systems and exist independently of logical Systems, then all attempts to prove or show that something is right or wrong are flawed. How is it possible to show that murder is bad or slavery is bad, if the very reasoning that we use for everyday life does not apply to morals?

Putting It All Together
Establishing Our First Consistent Moral System

With our new computer science tools in our toolkit, let's begin to construct our moral framework.

Ethics requires us to make *some* sort of value judgment. This is where our Axioms come into play. We want to distill what is good down to several key and finite assumptions that will not allow us to come up with Contradictory statements. At the same time, we need to choose enough Axioms such that we can rely on the System to Consistently and Deterministically tell us which actions are moral and which are not moral.

I think that it is fairly *self-evident* that "Human life is good" is a correct place to start.

This is a view shared by the Founding Fathers and serves as the bedrock of what many of us believe in. In the Declaration of Independence, Jefferson writes, "We

16

hold these truths to be *self-evident*, that all Men are created equal, that they are endowed by their Creator with certain unalienable Rights, that among these are *Life*, Liberty and the pursuit of Happiness . . ." (emphasis added by me).

The Founders believed that the rights to life and liberty were given to people by some higher being, such as God. In my moral System, I establish the idea (without trying to determine where that truth comes from) of the right to life as an Axiom—a truth that is self-evident.

However, the statement "Life is good" is too ambiguous. To come up with a consistent System, we need to be extremely careful when creating our Axioms. Let's frame our first Axiom like this:

I propose the **Do-No-Harm Axiom.**

To Harm another human life is bad
(and bad things must be prohibited)

Remember that this Axiom is an assumption that I believe is self-evident. Should someone disagree with this Axiom, there *cannot* be any meaningful dialogue between me and this person. Since we operate on different Axioms, that person would be operating outside of my moral framework, and, therefore, *no amount of vigorous debate* with this person will lead him to arrive at the same moral conclusions that I will. Imagine trying to debate with a suicide bomber at the dinner table. I foresee a rather explosive but ultimately fruitless conversation.

All other rules of my System can be carefully reasoned from here. Let us now carefully define "**Harm**." "**Harm**" means that, through an action you take, you have directly hurt someone physically, or you have directly made someone **Tangibly Worse Off** than he would have been had you not taken that action.

Things that this definition would immediately classify as bad include:

- Punching someone in the face
- Screaming loudly in someone's ear
- Touching someone without that person's permission

We will define an action that makes a person **Worse Off** as one that the same person would not have voluntarily taken. A person is **Worse Off** if you forcefully take a loaf of bread away from him. We call this action "stealing."

Even things that appear to be counterintuitive meet this definition. A person is **Worse Off** if you smack away a hamburger from his hands—even if eating burgers is not good for his health. That person must've judged that the enjoyment he gets from eating that burger outweighs the negative effects on his health. Otherwise, he would have chosen not to eat the burger.

Notice that **Worse Off** is *subjective* in the eyes of the person who could potentially be harmed. While a miserly person may not want to part with his loaf of bread, a more generous person who *voluntarily* gives away his bread to the poor is *not*, under this definition, **Worse Off**.

Tangible qualifies **Worse Off** by ensuring that the person who was made **Worse Off** can point to something measurable and observable as being lost or worsened. Bread taken away meets this criterion. A punch to the face also meets this criterion. Extraordinarily loud music at midnight that causes sleep deprivation to neighbors meets this criterion. Being called hurtful names, while rude, does not meet this criterion. Tears may be counted, but other than immeasurable "hurt feelings," there is nothing we can point to that shows something was lost.

Notice, also, how **Harm** needs to include some sort of action. While someone may be **Worse Off** because I did not give my bread to that person, it doesn't constitute **Harm** because I didn't do anything. If I weren't there, there would be no bread to give. Therefore, *not* doing an action to make someone better off is not the same as doing an action to make someone **Worse Off**. There is a difference between *preventing* (which is an action) someone from consuming bread in his possession, and *not giving* him bread (which is an inaction) to consume. A good test to see whether someone has taken an action is to imagine that person not being there to begin with. Does the outcome or situation change?

This concept is extraordinarily important. We must frame our moral System such that it is proscriptive, meaning that it is preventing some sort of action. It's not a coincidence that we chose "Do No Harm" as our Axiom rather than "Life Is Good." This is because "passive" Axioms that describe inaction as good or bad come with very severe consequences. Actions can always be prevented, but inaction can simply be a state of being. For example, while hunger and poverty are great problems that humanity should seek to eradicate, to make a moral judgment or Axiom that states "Poverty is bad (and bad things should be prohibited)," what we are effectively doing is condemning every single person on the planet to being bad until every single person on the planet eradicates poverty. While a noble goal, the implications of this means that everyone exists outside of the moral System, meaning we're *all* evil. This also means that the Axioms and laws that bind us together don't really apply anymore. Imagine telling a convicted murderer that it is against the law to spit on the floor. Why would he care? This prisoner already exists outside of the moral framework, as a result of his murdering someone. Therefore, such a System would be useless, because no one can comply with the System unless a certain a state of being is true.

LAWS OF NATURE AND THE STEALING-IS-BAD THEOREM

Now, I want to introduce a concept called a **Law of Nature**. These are laws that govern how the world works, like Newton's laws of gravity or his three laws of motion. No judgment call is needed, and no proof is necessary, as they are observable and are self-evident. To deny Laws of Nature is to reject reality as it is; it is as silly as saying that gravity doesn't exist. Debating with someone who denies Laws of Nature is just as fruitless as debating with someone with a different set of Axioms. No common ground can be established.

The first Law of Nature (**Humans-Must-Eat-to-Live LoN**) I will state is

In order to live, humans must consume.

This is obvious. "Consume" here does not mean only food, but food would be a great first example. If we don't eat, we die from starvation. If we don't live in a shelter, we die from exposure. If we don't wear warm clothes, we die from hypothermia. Consumption is not restricted to physical goods only. A person can also consume services. To live, I need to consult my doctor, to hire movers to lift heavy furniture, and to pay someone to provide electricity for my home. Therefore, if a human wants to live, he or she must want to consume. Therefore, we can deduce what I want to call the **Extended Humans-Must-Eat-to-Live Law of Nature.**

If a human wants to live, he must want to consume.

We are now ready to show our first moral Theorem. A deliberate action, therefore, that prevents someone from consuming something (which is Tangible) that he or she wants to consume (and would not voluntarily part with), is, by definition, making someone Tangibly Worse Off. In fact, this action also physically Harms the person's ability to live. The ability to consume is life itself; to take that away from someone constantly will eventually kill that person. Therefore, by the definition of Harm, we have shown

> **To take away from someone a good or service**
> **that he wants to consume Harms him.**

Therefore, alongside our Do-No-Harm Axiom, we can prove the **Stealing-Is-Bad Theorem**:

> **To take away from someone a good or**
> **service he wants to consume is bad.**

THE CREATOR-IS-THE-OWNER THEOREM

A second Law of Nature (**There Ain't No Such Thing as a Free Lunch LoN**) is

> **There can be no output for humans to consume**
> **if there is no human input (or production).**

This law is also known as TANSTAAFL[3] (a term borrowed from the economics book *Whatever Happened to Penny Candy?*). Just like the conservation of energy or the conservation of mass, something cannot come from nothing. Input must be introduced for there to be output to consume. If I want to sit on a chair, someone has to take wood, cut it up, and assemble it. If I want to wear clothes, someone needs to pick and process cotton, design the outfit, and create it. Even wild berries from a bush need to be foraged before we can eat them.

After a good or service is produced using human input, that good or service is naturally in the producer's possession. If I make a chair, that chair would be in my physical possession. For services, it's a bit more abstract, but it's still not a difficult concept to understand. If I am a doctor, the ability to provide health services lies within me. I, therefore, possess these services.

From the There-Ain't-No-Such-Thing-as-a-Free-Lunch LoN, we know that, if a good or service exists, someone must have created it. We also know that, at some point in time, this good or service was in the possession of its creator. What's more interesting is that the good or service will not have been in anyone else's possession *ever*, as the good or service did not exist before the creator's input.

Combine this with the Stealing-Is-Bad Theorem, and we can show that, should the creator want to consume his goods or services, to take away from the creator of a good or service is bad. Therefore, in this moral System, no one else is allowed to consume this good or service *except* for the creator! We now introduce a very important definition—**Ownership**.

A party (a person or a group of people) **Owns** goods and services when that party is permitted under this moral System to consume those goods and services. Notice that the party that Owns the goods or services is the *only* entity that is permitted under this moral System to consume those goods and services. Otherwise, by definition, other people who are allowed to consume those goods and services in our moral System will be part of that party.

Property are the goods and services that someone Owns.

Notice how I don't make any assumption on Property rights or Ownership. Ownership is a phenomenon that must naturally occur because of the There-Ain't-No-Such-Thing-as-a-Free-Lunch LoN and the Do-No-Harm Axiom! To deny that Property or Ownership exists means that we must start off with a different Axiom.

If someone agrees with my moral Axiom of Do No Harm (as the Laws of Nature cannot be disputed), Property must follow. Someone who denies Property needs to explain how, after a good is created and is in the possession of the creator, another person can morally take something away from the creator. Under our definitions of Harm and the Stealing-is-Bad Theorem, that person can't. Therefore, the only person who is allowed to consume this Property is the creator.

We have shown the **Creator-Is-the-Owner Theorem**:

The creator of a good or service is its rightful Owner.

Stated differently,

Goods and services are their creator's Property.

Using our new definitions, we can restate the Stealing-Is-Bad Theorem:

To take away someone's Property is bad.

THE VOLUNTARY TRADE THEOREM

What about goods and services we didn't create? Are we allowed to consume them? After all, I did not create the chair that I sit on, the spaghetti that I love eating, or the computer I use to type with. To make all of those myself, I'd have to be a wheat-grinding, pasta-making, computer-assembling, woodworking guru, and no one is that talented. However, there is nothing wrong with consuming these goods as long as we get these goods and services in a morally Consistent way.

We showed earlier that goods and services are their creator's property. Consider the following situation: A furniture-maker who makes a ton of chairs can't eat chairs but needs to eat food. A farmer needs chairs in order to rest after a strenuous harvest but has too many cabbages. The farmer proposes a **Trade**—an exchange of goods and services that is completely voluntary on the part of both parties. The farmer offers ten cabbages for one stool, and the furniture-maker agrees. Under our definition of **Harm**, both parties are *not* Tangibly Worse Off, because the exchange was *voluntary*. Stated in the opposite way, both parties are *better off* than or the same as they were before the exchange or Trade took place. Under this morally sanctioned transaction, possession of these goods and services has changed from their original creators to someone else. These people possess different goods after the trade, and no one else can steal these exchanged goods from them—the stool from the farmer and the cabbages from the furniture maker—without violating the Stealing-Is-Bad Theorem. By the definition of Property, the stool is now the farmer's Property and the cabbages, the furniture maker's.

Before we make our claim that this is the *only* method of moral Property transfer, we have to prove it. We'll do so via Proof by Contradiction:

Assume there exists an exchange of goods (we'll call it Exchange A) that is not a Trade but is morally good. By the definition of Trade, Exchange A (which is a not a Trade) is an exchange that did not happen voluntarily for either one or both parties. The effects of this exchange are Tangible, as this trade is observable and measurable. By the definition of Harm (defined as an action that wouldn't have been taken voluntarily and that causes a measurable effect), we have shown that one or both parties have been Harmed. By our Do-No-Harm Axiom, Exchange A is bad.

We now have an exchange (Exchange A) that is both good and bad—a Contradiction! Therefore, we have shown that there can be no exchanges of goods and services outside of Trade that is good.

We, thus, have proven our next Theorem, the **Voluntary Trade Theorem**.

The *only* way to morally change Ownership of a good or service is through voluntary Trade.

THE SLAVERY-IS-BAD THEOREM

I will define **Slavery** as "Forced input to a good or service." Slavery is forced and involuntary, usually with the threat of Harm should the Slave not comply. If I wanted to work as a grocery bagger, and I do so, by no means am I a Slave. If I didn't want to work as a grocery bagger, and someone forced me to bag groceries for him by either holding a gun to my head or by promising to lock me up in a prison if I refuse, this, by definition, is Slavery. We can see that, under this definition of Harm, Slavery makes the enslaved Tangibly Worse Off and therefore Harms them. Therefore, we can show directly that

Slavery is bad.

But another important Theorem we can show is the following:

Suppose a baker has a lot of bread. A lawmaker thinks that bread is an essential good and, therefore, should be distributed to everybody. He passes a law that says that bakers must contribute to society and "donate" a tenth of his bread to the poor. Those who don't comply are breaking the law and will be treated as criminals. Therefore, the baker, not wanting to be sent to prison or branded as an outlaw, complies. First, we see that the lawmaker's actions are wrong because, by definition, this is an involuntary transfer of Property (and the Voluntary-Trade Theorem shows this is bad). Second, by this definition, this is a form of forced labor or Slavery. Even though we are not taking away everything from the baker, we are still forcing an input of productivity into baked goods that we are systematically taking away from for other people's consumption. We have thus shown the **Systematic-Stealing-Is-Bad Theorem:**

> **Any form of (systematic) stealing of human input and productivity is bad.**

THE DO-WHAT-YOU-SAY THEOREM

Trade and exchanges need not happen only with goods and services we already own but also with goods and services to be exchanged or rendered in the future. For example, if a furniture-maker promises to give a farmer five chairs for ten cabbages and to deliver the chairs in one week, we'll show that to renege on this promise is bad. First, if the cabbages were paid upfront, we can see that this is a form of stealing, and Harm was certainly inflicted upon the farmer. However, even if cabbages were not paid upfront, a direct action was taken that has made the farmer Tangibly Worse Off. Had the furniture-maker not been there, he would not have been able to make a promise that he would eventually not fulfill in the future. The cabbage farmer was relying on the promise of the five chairs. Maybe the farmer was going to hire four workers who needed them, or maybe he had to set aside ten cabbages for the Trade, and now he is unable to sell them. Regardless, the cabbage farmer was Harmed because he would not have chosen such an action be taken (the breaking of promises), and the breaking of such promise can definitely cause measurable effects on the farmer. This shows that:

To renege on an agreement Harms someone.

Therefore, along with the Do-No-Harm Axiom, we show the **Do-What-You-Say Theorem**,

To renege on an agreement is bad.

HANDLING THOSE WHO DO NOT ABIDE BY OUR MORAL SYSTEM

Everything we proved earlier are rules that show what is moral and what is not. However, our System is still not finished. While it seems Deterministic so far, it is not Exhaustive. It does not provide a road map for what is allowed to those who break the rules of our moral System.

To get a better sense of what we've historically done, consider the Wild West. In the Wild West, those who broke the law were called Outlaws. They were outside of the protection of the law, and, therefore, almost anything could be done to them. The state or a judge would, and did, place bounties for their capture or death.[4]

There is no road map or method for our current moral System to handle people who do bad or prohibited things. We must make a *judgment call* for what is a moral way to handle immoral or bad people. We now need to expand and introduce a new Axiom to our moral System to handle bad people. We could start from anywhere. We could immediately condemn those people to death. Anybody who stole from anyone or attempted to punch someone would be immediately executed. This, however, is a judgment I can confidently say most people would call "unfair" or "immoral." Therefore, I feel a reasonably self-evident way to handle bad people is the following:

Those who commit immoral acts shall not be protected by our moral System until they have made whole their victims. For victims they are unable to make whole, they shall engage in activities that will allow them to make whole their victims as much as possible.

This concept of handling people who are immoral differs from what we experience today, but it seems self-evident. Most criminals today spend time in prison. The problem with prison is that the damage done to the victims will never be made whole. If someone steals a loaf of bread and is caught, his victim will be much better off receiving payment for the goods stolen as well as an extra payment for the time and effort wasted catching the thief. This system also has the benefit of assigning different value, based on the severity of the crimes. The heavier the crime, the more that needs to be restored. Even victims of murder can benefit from a criminal who is put to work to try to restore as much as possible to the families of his victims rather than just sitting in a prison cell.

Although this proposal seems radical, restitution was a familiar concept to many societies in the past.[4] Regardless, the purpose of this Axiom is simply a way to handle people who do not abide by our moral System. It is an assumption, but it does not fundamentally change what is permitted within our system. Therefore, for the purposes of making my moral System Exhaustive, I will refer to this catch-all Axiom as the **What-to-Do-With-Bad-People Axiom**.

With those few Axioms and Theorems, we've now established our first simple (but rather powerful) ethical System. For the rest of the book, we'll refer to this ethical System as the "Free-Market System."

Well-Intentioned (but Contradictory)
Socialist Attempts to Expand
on This Moral System

The Free-Market System is not particularly new or interesting. Even those without a formal ethical System know that stealing, slavery, and murder are wrong. After all, most of those Axioms and Theorems are encapsulated in what we teach children today. "The Golden Rule" of doing unto others that which you would want them to do to you does a pretty good job of describing most—but not all—of what we have said about the Free-Market System.

The Free-Market System, however, is quite limited and is so intentionally. It says nothing about fairness, or saving lives, or all the other things that we inherently believe to be right, such as being a Good Samaritan. People often confuse individual values with a set of morals. Unfortunately, trying to systematically include many of these values in a shared, consistent moral code is difficult, if not impossible. Perhaps the biggest opponents to the Free-Market System are modern-day liberals, socialists, or progressives. These groups of people, while they have a range of different and nuanced views, have one unifying principle in common: They share the belief that society is morally required to help provide some sort of assistance to others and that *not* to provide people with help is immoral. For the purpose of clarity, the term I have chosen to address this group of people is "socialists." In the next part of the book, we will show a few common but Contradictory attempts that modern socialists make to expand upon the Free-Market System.

A CLOSER LOOK AT THE KEY DEFINITION OF HARM

Before we go on trying to show why socialist Systems are Contradictory Systems, we first need to take a look at how I have defined key terms earlier. The purpose of these precise definitions is for them to capture what most people would think these words mean, to be as unambiguous as possible, but most importantly, so that they don't lead to Contradictions within our system. Let's take a look at some key definitions in closer detail:

Harm—Through an action that you take, you have directly hurt someone physically, or you have directly made someone Tangibly Worse Off than he would have been had you not taken that action.

Tangibly Worse Off—An action that makes a person Worse Off is one that this same person would not have voluntarily taken. Tangible qualifies Worse Off by ensuring that the person who was made Worse Off can point to something measurable and observable as being lost or worsened.

Few people would dispute that physically hurting someone or encroaching on someone's body constitutes Harm. However, why does Harm need to make someone Tangibly Worse Off? Can the definition be made stricter or looser?

Let's try to make the definition of Harm stricter and define Harm to include only physical assault or improper touching of one's physical person. This means that stealing is not immoral. As long as I don't touch someone or punch someone, I can always raid granaries, steal lunches from fridges, and drive away with my neighbor's car. But why can't it be moral? We can't just say that it's obvious, since all obvious judgment calls must be made in our Axioms.

Let's assume that stealing is moral so long as I don't touch someone. If you are sleeping at night, and I come to your house and steal all your food, money, phones, and every physical thing that you aren't touching, it won't be long before you're either dead from starvation, thirst, exposure, cold, and so forth. Essentially, my actions have killed you. Even on the off chance they don't, they certainly have physically affected you (you are hungrier, weaker, sicker, or colder). This now meets the first criterion for Harm. So now stealing can't be moral—a Contradiction.

We can also try to make the definition of "Harm" looser. Instead of Tangibly Worse Off, let's just say Worse

Off. The problem with not qualifying Worse Off in a way that a third party could observe or measure is that since Worse Off is subjective, anything can make anyone Worse Off. Assume I don't like the color of your house. Does that make me Worse Off, and are you in the wrong for painting your house that color? Am I justified in bulldozing your house down? Worse, let's say I don't like *you* as a person. Your being alive makes me Worse Off because I have an irrational hatred toward you. What do we do in this situation? Can I kill you? Can you kill me in self-defense? Is anyone left inside the moral System when everyone can potentially be Harming someone without even knowing it? We're left in a situation in which everyone is Harmed, and the actions to remedy those Harms lead to more Harm—an infinite cycle of Contradictions. Therefore, the current definition of Harm is as specific and self-evident as it can be.

SOCIALIST ATTEMPT AT EXPANDING THIS MORAL FRAMEWORK #1

Now we have a taste of what kinds of ridiculous Contradictions we can get when we use sloppy definitions of key terms. Let's take a look at several ways many socialists or progressives seek to expand upon this moral framework that ultimately lead to Contradictions.

Most socialists will generally agree that "Do No Harm" is a good and ethical Axiom. Their biggest complaint with the Free-Market System is that they think it's too harsh or restrictive. Typically, they believe that it is immoral for humans to let other humans in need suffer, and, therefore, they want some sort of minimum standard of living for everyone.

Many socialists (and conservatives, for that matter) take issue with people not being able to survive or not having access to basic necessities. Any empathetic human being would be concerned about this. However, socialists go one step further by saying that people have a right to clean water, to food, to electricity, and to education. Most proponents of liberty would have no issue with the statement above, but, due to the Laws of Nature, the addition of these rights to our Free-Market System has some very dangerous implications.

Instead of adding a bunch of specific rights to our Axioms, let's try to encapsulate the general idea of the right to basic necessities into a moral Axiom via the addition of a new Axiom—**The Leave-No-Person-Behind Axiom**.

It is bad to Allow someone to live below a Minimum Standard of Living.

We need to define two key terms—"**Allow**" and "**Minimum Standard of Living**."

Let's first define "**Minimum Standard of Living**." Immediately, we see a glaring issue. Unlike the definition of "Harm," the definition of "Minimum Standard of

Living" is not self-evident or easily agreed upon. We'll try to define Minimum Standard of Living as best we can, in a way that most socialists would probably agree with.

It's obvious that the needs of people are different. A diabetic needs insulin, while others do not. Big, muscular people need more calories compared to their smaller peers. To capture this dynamic, let's propose that the needs of the people are defined by the people in need themselves. We'll prove that this definition does not work.

We'll provide the following Counter-Example: I am a jealous person, and I "need" my neighbor's car, house, and maybe his or her kids! In fact, everything in the world should belong to me, I claim. I am a person in need who needs my neighbor's *everything*.

Clearly, this is not reasonable. First, it is impracticable. If everything belongs to me, everyone else in the world would die from starvation, and this will Harm every single living thing in existence—a massive Contradiction. Second, socialists would claim that this person clearly does not truly need his neighbor's car and kids. While I would agree that this is probably not a good definition of "need," this point illustrates that "need" cannot be defined by the person in need.

Therefore, we require a third party (hopefully, a reasonable and benevolent third party) to define it. Socialists would claim that this is not necessary. *Society* would define it. But what, specifically, is society? Society in this instance *cannot* be everyone. The person who is needy *cannot* define what **Needy** is because of the Contradiction we showed earlier. Therefore, the largest society can be in this context is everyone else *excluding* the person, or people, in need, which we will call the **Needy**. This third party has to be the **Not-Needy**. However, if we try to define what Needy and Non-Needy are, we realize we don't have the necessary tools to do so. We are unable to define Needy and Not-Needy before we define what Minimum Standard of Living is! But to define what Minimum Standard of Living is, we need to know what Needy and Not-Needy are! This is a dilemma.

The way socialists attempt to solve this dilemma is by blurring the lines between Needy and Not-Needy and to avoid this problem altogether. Let's say there is a process in which we can get a reasonable and fair third party (perhaps by an election). This process will ensure (we're not sure how yet, but assume we can do this) that this third party—we don't know whether this third party is Needy or Not-Needy—will not define his or her own needs in an unreasonable way. Let this third party define what Minimum Standard of Living is. We'll call this third party the **Representative**. Note that the Representative does not have to be an organization that has sole power to make executive decisions. It could very well be a simple democracy, in which *people vote on* what the definition of Minimum Standard of Living is. In this case, however, the *majority* would be the Representative.

We'll have the Representative define Minimum Standard of Living as a "basket of goods and services to ensure life." This basket of goods and services will include lifesaving medicines and doctors' visits, and a minimum amount of food tailored to the caloric needs of people (again, defined by a third party—maybe by an expert doctor or nutritionist). Let's say that a basket of goods and services is **Essential** to a person; if it's not consumed, it will cause death for that person. There are still issues with this definition, but let's continue on this train of thought for now.

We have now defined, as best we can, Minimum Standard of Living.

Minimum Standard of Living is a basket of Essential goods and services, the contents of which is decided by a Representative.

Next, let's define "**Allow**." Again, we see something very dangerous that we alluded to earlier on. No matter how we define "Allow," it is not proscriptive. "Allow" is a verb that implies a state of being or inaction on the part of everyone who agrees to this moral System. The most obvious definition of Allow is that it means inaction by someone, in this case, the Not-Needy, that causes the state of someone else (in this case, the Needy) to be unchanged. In other words, Allow means inaction on the part of the Not-Needy to help the Needy.

Therefore, we restate **The Leave-No-Person-Behind Axiom.**

> **It is bad for the Not-Needy (defined by a Representative) not to provide a basket of Essential goods and services, the contents of which is decided by a Representative, to the Needy (defined by a Representative).**

We now have a Contradiction. If the Not-Needy do not want to give away their goods and services to the Needy, does this not constitute Harm? This contradicts our Do-No-Harm Axiom.

There is no way around it, unless we try to redefine what "Harm" means. Our earlier definition of Harm is quite reasonable, and we have already shown numerous but failed attempts to loosen or tighten the definition of Harm that leads to a Contradiction. The one—and perhaps only—way socialists can redefine Harm is to add an exception to the definition of Harm, like so:

"Harm" means that, through an action that you take, you have directly hurt someone physically, or you have directly made someone Tangibly Worse Off than he would have been had you not taken that action *except* when the Not-Needy are being made Tangibly Worse Off by providing for the Needy to be better off. The Needy and Not-Needy are *defined by a Representative.*

Without this redefinition of Harm, the Not-Needy, by definition, are Slaves of the Needy. And we have already shown that Slavery is bad.

That last phrase in italics (about the Representative) has to be there because we have shown that defining Needy and Not-Needy is a human construct and can't be done independently without this third party. This definition of Harm is *not* self-evident. Does any English dictionary define the word "harm" with a case-by-case process? Even a murderer can be harmed using any reasonable standard definition of that word. To put it more bluntly, someone may *deserve* to get his ass kicked, but that fact does not make that action any less of an ass-kicking.

Ignoring this issue and with this exception in hand, the moral System appears to be Consistent now. However, in trying to make the system Consistent, we have done something terrible—our system is not Exhaustive, nor is it Deterministic!

It's extremely easy to show how it is not Exhaustive, as our next example shows how this "System" fails when we bump into the There-Ain't-No-Such-Thing-as-a-Free-Lunch Law of Nature.

Consider the theoretical example below: The world is efficient enough to produce only 100 bowls of rice a day. You have a population of 1,000 people. In our hypothetical world, if a person does not eat one bowl of rice a day, that person will die from starvation. We can see that this is a situation that this moral System cannot handle. There is no solution in this instance that can ensure a Minimum Standard of Living for everyone. Therefore, using these Axioms, the passive nature of the word "Allow" rears its ugly head. *No one* can be good in this system. If everyone is a criminal in (or a violator of) this moral System, the System is useless.

This isn't just a theoretical exercise. We do not have unlimited goods and services in the world. The total output of the world is limited by how productive the average person is. The purchasing power parity-adjusted GDP per capita of the world right now is roughly $11,433[5] with a total GDP (PPP) of approximately $135 trillion[6] (our 100 bowls of rice a day). This is a hard limit. This means that the cost of all the goods and services that people can possibly consume per year (never mind the amount of money that needs to be reinvested to maintain the equipment we use to produce goods efficiently), on average, cannot exceed $11,433. This also states that the cost of the maximum amount of Essential goods that can be distributed to everyone is, at most, $11,433 per year. The moment anyone tries to consume $11,434 of goods and services, that person will realize that the grocery shelves are empty and that every single surgeon or barber is occupied, as there is nothing left. Now, the question becomes: "Is $11,434 per person enough to subsist on?" Many would say, "Yes." However, I believe that is a spurious claim, which, when examined closely, few socialists would agree with or would actually be willing to practice themselves. In the United

States, fewer than 13% of the population earn less than that amount.[7] The United States is one of the wealthiest and most productive nations in the world, with a GDP per capita of roughly $65,000 per year and a total domestic output of roughly $20 trillion per year.[8] Our definition of "poverty" is an income of less than $12,760 a year.[9] Does the average socialist really believe that earning $1,000 less than the United States' definition of poverty is enough for the average person in the world to enjoy a minimum standard of living? While it is extremely difficult to strictly show that $11,433 is not enough for everyone to enjoy a minimum standard of living, there is ample evidence to construct a reasonable Counter-Example to show that, for at least one person in that pool, $11,433 is not enough.

The cost of certain kinds of treatment for leukemia ranges from $25,000 to $100,000 per patient[10], which is already higher than $11,433.

Some may say that the cost of treatment is artificially high because of prices set by hospitals and doctors. Unfortunately, that is not the case, as the average operating margin (meaning the percentage difference between revenue and expenses) for U.S. hospitals is roughly 8%.[11] This means the *economic cost* of certain types of treatments of leukemia is higher than the maximum possible basket of goods and services of $11,433 we can possibly provide to everyone.

A socialist may claim we should then give the leukemia patient more, but that can do only one thing. If someone gets more than the average of goods and services produced, then someone must get less, since we are restricted by the amount of goods and services produced, and that number is a hard limit.

The simple fact of the matter is that we are not productive enough for everyone to afford lifesaving cancer treatment. We can consume only what we produce. If many people get cancer (38% of people can expect to get cancer in their lifetimes[12]) but we can't afford to treat them all, what happens? *Everyone is bad*, as there is *nothing* we can do to provide this Minimum Standard of Living to everyone. Our "System" is stuck.

This does not imply that people should just condemn the less fortunate to living a miserable and sickly life. Later in the book, we will focus on the economic implications of the example above. For now, it clearly shows that, if people are not productive enough in the aggregate to feed themselves, no scheme for redistribution of wealth will make it possible for everyone to eat. It helps us focus on the real problems: How do we make all people productive enough to afford lifesaving cancer treatment, and how can we be productive enough to bring down the economic costs of cancer treatment?

Our System is also not Deterministic. It can change, depending on what the Representative thinks or feels, or on who the Representative is. There is no Consistency in the System. If the System chooses another Representative the next day, suddenly the definitions of Minimum Standard of Living will change. A set of actions that was good yesterday is suddenly bad today, when nothing changed except for the *opinion* of the Representative or the Representative *chosen*. We have what essentially is a moral code that can change at the *whim* of the Representative. This is not a System, and it is certainly not an ethical System.

SOCIALIST ATTEMPT AT EXPANDING THIS MORAL FRAMEWORK #2

There is nothing that a socialist can do to make this "System" Deterministic, because a Representative has to be involved, and the Representative or the Representative's values can change. To try to make their "System" Exhaustive, socialists revise the Leave-No-Person-Behind Axiom to the following:

> **It is bad for the Not-Needy (defined by a Representative) not to provide a basket of Essential goods and services to the Needy (defined by a Representative) when we still have Not-Needy.**

Now, the "System" is Exhaustive. But what have we done? The only way for *anyone* not to be bad is, essentially, if either *everyone* can meet the Minimum Standard of Living or if *no one* can meet the Minimum Standard of Living. Nature does not provide for us, and, so, unless we are fortunate enough to produce enough for everyone to enjoy the Minimum Standard of Living, every single person who adheres to this moral System will perpetually be in a situation in which *no one* meets the Minimum Standard of Living.

Let's take a look at the things we had to do in order to shoehorn this Axiom in. We had to change the definition of Harm to exclude the Not-Needy as determined by a Representative. We had to define Minimum Standard of Living as a basket of Essential goods and services provided to everyone who meets the criteria for "Needy," decided by a Representative. It's now Exhaustive, but it sure isn't Deterministic. This "Representative" rears his ugly head everywhere.

WHAT THE AXIOMS END UP BECOMING—A DIFFERENT KIND OF MORAL FRAMEWORK

While, on the surface, it appears that we have just expanded the set of Axioms with the No-Person-Left-Behind Axiom to my Free-Market Axioms, upon closer inspection, we have changed the entire Axiomatic System entirely.

Let's look at the two key additions or revisions:

It is bad for the Not-Needy (defined by a Representative) not to provide a basket of Essential goods and services to the Needy (defined by a Representative) when we still have Not-Needy.

"Harm" means that, through an action that you take, you have directly hurt someone physically, or you have directly made someone Tangibly Worse Off than he would have been had you not taken that action, *except* when the Not-Needy are being made Tangibly Worse Off by providing for the Needy to be better off. The Needy and Not-Needy are *defined by a Representative.*

Focusing on the term "Not-Needy," this definition can change however the Representative sees fit. You can be "Harmed" at any particular time of day, so long as you are defined to be Not-Needy. One day you are allowed to be Harmed, and one day you are not, as defined by the Representative. Therefore, the Do-No-Harm Axiom actually doesn't do *anything*. It looks like it is there to prevent people from hurting others, but the special group that is allowed to be hurt (the Not-Needy) is forever malleable and changing!

What the introduction of this Axiom does is make this System an Exhaustive—but not Deterministic—"System" in disguise. Its only Axiom is:

Might Is Right

The **Mighty** are the people who choose who the Representative is. We can easily see how this System is Exhaustive. A new situation comes along—is it right or wrong? It is whatever the Mighty say it is, whether it be a dictator, commissar, President, or democratic majority. Is this Axiom really what socialists believe is self-evident? They claim "No," but this follows with any introduction of a Leave-No-Person-Behind Axiom.

SOCIALIST ATTEMPT AT EXPANDING THIS MORAL FRAMEWORK #3

I won't go into detail, but the logic above is still valid, no matter what kind of Leave-No-Person-Behind Axiom you introduce. It could be any **Positive Right**, such as the right to water, to food, or to education, and you could go down the same logical path to show that the system devolves into Might Is Right.

A QUICK WAY TO CHECK THE VALIDITY OF MORAL PRINCIPLES

A very effective way of testing the validity—not of the *idea* but of the *principle*—of certain statements is to suggest an extreme statement with the same principle. Consider the United Nations Universal Declaration of Human Rights. A couple of articles are modeled very similarly to the United States Constitution[13]:

Article 4) No one shall be held in slavery or servitude

Article 9) No one shall be subjected to arbitrary arrest, detention, or exile

These are what philosophers refer to as **Negative Rights**, which means that these are rights that everyone already has by nature and that can be taken away only by being Harmed or encroached upon by another person. People are not Slaves until they are made ones by their captors. People are free to roam about and cannot arbitrarily arrest themselves. The United States Constitution primarily deals with Negative Rights. Negative Rights do not have scales or metrics that can be changed and are as extreme as they can possibly be.

The United Nations Declaration begins to differ when it introduces **Positive Rights**. Positive Rights are rights that need to be provided by someone. Consider a section of Article 26:

> **Everyone has the right to education.**
> **Education shall be free, at least in the**
> **elementary and fundamental stages.**

Senator Bernie Sanders echoes that statement by stating that we should "make public colleges, universities, and trade schools free for all."[14]

The problem with Positive Rights is that it requires action to provide these rights. By the definition of Positive Right, no Positive Right can *ever be free* in the economic sense. It can be free for *some*, but that can only mean that someone else is bearing the *cost*. Teachers and school supplies, unlike the right not to be arbitrarily arrested, do not exist without human input. If there are not enough teachers or school supplies, there is no way to ensure that everyone gets an education. Will we force people to teach and force people to provide school supplies for others? Is that not a form of systematic Slavery?

A good way to test the validity of the statement as a moral principle is to bring the statement to extremes:

To make everyone better off, why don't we suggest an even better human right? Why don't we say that every person has the right to twenty 30,000-square-foot mansions, a two-hour workday, a three-day workweek, and a tennis court? In principle, is there any difference between making education free and making water free, or any good or service free? They are, after all, goods and services that require human input. This example clearly is ludicrous. No one would agree that the above is a fundamental human right.

People can claim that education is different because it is more important. But then they would meet the same issue of defining "important." In other words, they would make the argument that education is an Essential good, which will need to be defined by a Representative. The arguments will then mirror what we have shown above.

SIGNIFICANCE OF WHAT WE'VE SHOWN

We have shown that, with the introduction of a well-intentioned Leave-No-Person-Behind Axiom, we *must* introduce a Representative whose power comes from defining who the Needy and Not-Needy are, without any self-evident framework and whose presence is required for the "System" to function. Good and evil are as defined by the Representative, and it implies that what is right and what is wrong is a matter of human opinion. Notions that people are created equal are gone.

I think even the staunchest of socialists believe in equality under the law and that "All Men are Created Equal." Most socialists I know have issues with powerful businesses and lobbyists buying our elections at the expense of the poorer working class. However, if their "System" requires a Representative to define "Needy" and "Not-Needy," which requires Might to be Right, it fundamentally shows that their system is not about equality. It is about power and who has it. They just happen to be rooting for another team.

WHY CONSISTENCY IS SO IMPORTANT

Earlier we mentioned the theoretical implications of an Inconsistent System with the Principle of Explosion and how it renders all statements true and false at the same time. An Inconsistent Moral System has many dangerous real-world implications.

First, it means that any action can be right or wrong at the same time. People generally feel that it is okay for morals to not be "black-and-white" and that values of what is right or wrong will always be a pendulum that swings back and forth. However, why would morals be different from any other System we are used to? If moral Systems cannot be Consistent, there is no concept of right or wrong, and everything is based on whim. Loose and contradictory moral thinking is what allows for people to justify doing evil things with good intentions and to use immoral actions as a means to an end. Pol Pot, Lenin, and the Unabomber all killed for their versions of a better world and used killing as a means to their "moral" ends. Consistency forces us to think things out thoroughly and not to allow for exceptions that lead to such atrocities.

Second, it allows for certain statements or actions to be right for some but wrong for others. That is true inequality—inequality under the law. Oppressors can oppress only if they are guided by a different set of rules. Be wary of Systems that have to carve out different types of people to be subject to different sets of rules. They invariably lead to Contradictions and oppression.

WHERE DOES THAT LEAVE US?

When discussing with socialists, the fundamental question we have to ask them is this:

Unless they can find a hole in the reasoning listed above, then it must follow that the moral "System" they propose is built upon the Axiom of Might Is Right. The final question to ask is this:

Do *you* believe this is self-evident and fair?

If Might Is Right is truly what proponents of socialism believe in, then our starting Axioms are different—there is no room for discourse. It is up to those who believe in freedom and equality to do everything they are morally permitted to do (within their System) to protect their own right to life, liberty, and the pursuit of happiness.

PART II

CREATING AN ECONOMIC MENTAL MODEL:

*Problems of the World and How
We Overcome Them*

The Importance of a Mental Model

Now that we have established a theoretical way to view ethics and morals, this section of the book will focus on the more practical matters of the world.

Since we are leaving the strict world of definitions and formal logic, from now on, **boldfaced** words will just be terms that I want to emphasize and want the reader to think critically about. If the terms need more explanation, I will try my best to do so.

This part of the book explores the reasons why certain systems of ethics exist and how ethics is centered around how the world works. The three biggest issues I see with many young people today when discussing ethics and economics are the following:

1. They do not have a rudimentary understanding of how the world works economically or a mental economic model that they can rely on.

2. They fail to see how many of the actions they take affect the current system or how things are interconnected. A good model is one that **connects** a bunch of ideas together.

3. They do not have a sense of proportion of how far we have come and take for granted the miracles of human achievement today. In trying to address today's issues, they tear apart the things that enabled us to achieve these miracles.

A SENSE OF PROPORTION

Before we address the first two points, let's briefly discuss what it means to have a sense of proportion. To live and prosper, people must strive to overcome certain laws of nature. The world is an unforgiving place. Famine, war, disease, and thugs threaten our way of life every step of the way. At the same time, we must not forget that the world also offers us the means to overcome many of those challenges and that humans have certainly come a long way.

As Milton Friedman used to say, "We must have a sense of proportion."[15] The GDP of England in the 1300s is estimated to be roughly $6 million in today's money.[16] The GDP per capita of the average person in the United States is roughly $65,000 per year. This means, assuming that the king of England owned everything in the country back then, which is a stretch, 100 average citizens of the United States would have a combined wealth of more than that of the king of England. In the eyes of a common Englishman from the middle ages, we *all* live like kings. The poor person who has a yearly income of $25,000 per year in America is 67 times wealthier than the average ancient Roman citizen, who was the envy of the world at the time.[17]

A person who flips burgers or mows lawns or stacks books for a $7/hour wage can easily buy $100 worth of groceries a week; that would have taken an average medieval farmer three months to save.[16] The fraction of income that the average American spends today on basic goods and services has gone from 55% to a smidge over 30% in just a matter of eight decades.[18] By earning more, not only do modern humans live longer and healthier lives, but they also are able to enjoy spending their spare time in the sunshine, playing with their kids, or pursuing hobbies.

Change in U.S. Spending on Basics As A Share of Disposable Income Over Time[18]

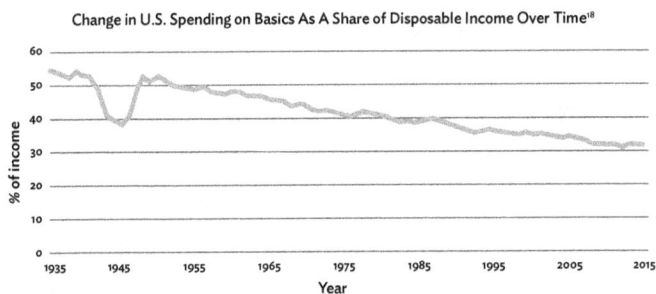

However, these days, many people forget the great strides made by humans that people from as little as 100 years ago would have thought impossible. Taking for granted the miracles of human ingenuity and forgetting the inputs required for production, they see corporations with large cash balances and think that the way to reduce poverty is to tax businesses and redistribute wealth to the less fortunate. In principle, it is no different from looking at endless rows of shelves stocked with food at the grocery store. One may think that the solution for ending world hunger is that, as long as there's food on the shelf, there's plenty to go around for everyone and that we should distribute it to anyone who is hungry. They seem to have lost the curiosity about where things come from and **how these things are made**.

Many people claim they know how things are made. After all, anyone can tune in to Discovery Channel's *How It's Made* and see rolls of paper being printed on massive machines or how machines drop cranberries onto conveyor belts to pick out the fresh ones from the rotten ones. However, they think that's where it stops. Their model of production stops at the boundaries of the factory floor and is siloed off. It ignores the bigger picture. What they really need is a show called *How It's Really Made* that tells us about the forces and mechanisms that put those machines on those factory floors and the system that helped assemble a well-trained workforce to operate the machines. Where did the **salaries** come from? Where did the initial **capital investment** for the machines come from? Where did the **idea of an assembly line** come from? The key is to understand **not how we produce a**

certain item but rather the **conditions necessary for production as a whole.**

THE DANGER OF SILOED MODELS

Models that do not connect bodies of ideas together can be dangerous. There's a very memorable scene from the movie *Saving Private Ryan* that drives this point home. In the famous "FUBAR scene," Captain Miller's team meets an American pilot whose glider has crashed. He explains to Captain Miller that, because his glider was carrying a high-ranking brigadier general, "a couple of geniuses" decided, without telling the captain, to weld a couple of steel plates onto the plane to protect the general from ground fire. These "geniuses," who had the best intentions at heart, had two disjointed models. One, gliders fly. Two, steel plates stop bullets. Without truly understanding the model of flying, they took the most direct approach in trying to solve the problem of protecting the general. Unfortunately, by welding plates onto the glider, the pilot was unable to maneuver his glider properly. He crashed and killed not only the general but also the vast majority of his crew. His co-pilot was decapitated.

This deadly outcome could have easily been avoided in two ways. Had the welders known the physics of a glider, they would have known not to load the aircraft with too much weight. That, however, is not very realistic. Skilled metal workers and welders most likely wouldn't have doctorates in aerodynamics or expertise in aircraft design. The best way to avoid a disaster like this is to have a **sense of proportion** and the curiosity and humility to ask yourself, "A glider is a complex machine, designed by some very smart people. There must be a reason why airplanes do not have thick metal plates all around to protect the people inside from gunfire. The solution of welding plates seems too easy. Have other people tried this before? If not, *why* haven't other people tried this before?"

The economy, similarly, is just as complex, if not more complex, than an aircraft. The problems we see today are obvious, such as famine, homelessness, and poverty. However, socialists who view the word in a disjointed manner propose solutions that exacerbate the problems. For example, people see high rental costs as a cause of homelessness, only to find out that rent control helps only those who are fortunate enough to get rent-controlled housing. San Francisco, one of the most expensive places in the U.S. to live, implements rent control. Because landlords are capped with regard to what they can charge, they are not incentivized to maintain or buy more rental units. Instead, they were incentivized to demolish old buildings or convert units into condominiums. As the supply of rentable units dropped, rents increased dramatically, harming those the city had aimed to help.[19]

As the complexity of the world continues to increase, many people forget to take a step back and to think about how the world works as a whole. Their mental models are unable to link the laws of nature, the ingenious solutions we have come up with to tackle them, and how they fit in. To begin to understand how we have overcome many of our problems, we need to first know what the problems are.

The Fundamental Problem
Two Pesky Laws of Nature

The first law of nature we are beholden to is

To live, humans must consume.

Life is a precarious balancing act and an interplay of a bunch of systems within an organism. A very specific environment is necessary for our bodies to function and to allow the pumps in our cells to move proteins and molecules about, providing important organs with nutrients and oxygen. To survive, we need a stable environment and a continuous source of energy. For these cells to function, the environment cannot be too cold or too warm. In fact, the temperature must be 37 degrees Celsius; a variation of just 3 to 4 degrees would kill us. We need to be protected from outside forces that could cause irreparable physical trauma to our bodies. We need to continuously replenish our body's energy supply with foods and liquids. Nature, unfortunately, is not a nice climate-controlled bubble, nor is it a magical cornucopia, with manna raining down from the heavens. While we have everything we need to survive, action is required to gain access to these life-giving resources.

That is the **Law of Nature** that governs all forms of life, from the single-cell protozoa to the largest of wildebeests. Sustaining life requires action—action to change the environment we are in and action to find sources of nourishment. We all must consume to live.

The second law of nature we are beholden to is

**There can be no output for humans to consume
if there is no human input (or production).**

Output is another way of saying "what we produce." The production that we eat and use for our survival is what we consume. Putting on our economist's hat, we can restate the second law of Nature with a mathematical formula:

Consumption ≤ Production + Savings

The above states that you cannot consume more than you have produced and saved. Too often, people focus only on the left side of the equation. As consumers, that is what most of us see in our everyday lives—consumption. If we are hungry, we must spend money to eat. If we need to travel, we go to the dealership to get a car. Similarly, when we see homelessness, we think about providing them with a small apartment to live in. After all, we see plenty of homes to go around.

What most of us do not see is production and the steps required to bring these goods and services to the market. More importantly, most people who work in our complex modern service economy, providing important services such as accounting, data analytics, nursing, and banking, are so far removed from the final product that they do not realize how they fit into the great production supply chain.

The second law of nature is much easier to comprehend in a simpler agrarian society, and I suspect that's why so many people disillusioned with modern society look upon those "simpler" times with an unjustified idealism and nostalgia (running a farm is a terrible, back-breaking, relentless physical activity). In a simpler, agrarian society, it is clear that if you don't grow enough food, no matter what you do to divide the food, people will starve.

An old Chinese story best encapsulates the conclusions we make when we forget the second law of nature:

Around 300 AD, during the reign of Emperor Hui in the Jin Dynasty, officials begged the Emperor to address the terrible poverty and famine of the people. They told Emperor Hui that the common Chinese man did not have rice to eat. The Emperor simply replied, "So, why don't they eat meat?"[20] (There is a more-popular apocryphal story of Marie Antoinette saying, "Let them eat cake!" when asked about the starving peasants in France.)

What is the Emperor missing here? He knows that humans suffer when they don't consume the things they need. His most direct and natural response is that the solution should be to let them consume. After all, nobody is stopping them from eating meat. What he and many socialists today focus on is consumption, because, oblivious to how the world works, they take production for granted. There is no output without input. You can't consume what isn't produced. You can't give starving people any food or meat if the grocery shelves are empty. Somebody has to grow that food.

The Fundamental Solution
Produce, Produce, Produce

How do humans overcome this fundamental problem? They toil and struggle and sweat for one purpose: to produce and produce and produce. To consume and live and thrive, we must produce. From the bread we eat to the music we listen to, someone had to have taken the time to make these things. Humans wake up every morning knowing that they need to sow the seeds for tomorrow's meal, to build the shelters that will protect them from the elements and from predators, and to work for the luxuries they enjoy in order to make their lives worth living.

To produce, humans have two main tools at their disposal: their being (body and mind) and the tools they have available. Economists like to call these two things **labor**, which I will call "L" in formulae, and **capital**, which I will call "K." In mathspeak, we like to say that production is a *function* (let's call this function *f*) of these two inputs.

$$\text{Production} = f(\text{L, K})$$

Labor consists of your mind and our body. It can be your physical strength that you use to plow the fields or the skills you acquired in school to operate the complex machines and computers for your work. You can improve labor differently, depending on the type of job you do. If you are a farmer, you could work out to become stronger, or, if you are a business analyst, you could attend graduate school and learn better skills. These improvements make you a better **laborer**. This is what most of mankind relied on in an agrarian society, before the Industrial Revolution, in order to improve their lives. After the Industrial Revolution, we saw massive improvements in productivity due to an influx of capital and innovation that has made humans significantly more productive.

Putting the "Capital"
in "Capitalism"

What is "capital"? We hear businessmen, politicians, financiers, bankers, and economists throw this word around all the time. Capital is, in its most basic form, the tools we use to produce. Capital is the machines on the factory floor, the shears in a gardener's hands, and American Airline's multi-billion-dollar fleet of Boeing and Airbus jets. More abstractly, it is also the funds that allow firms and businesses to open factories and buy trucks and planes. Therefore, in this more abstract definition, almost everything is capital.

INPUTS

OUTPUT/PRODUCTION

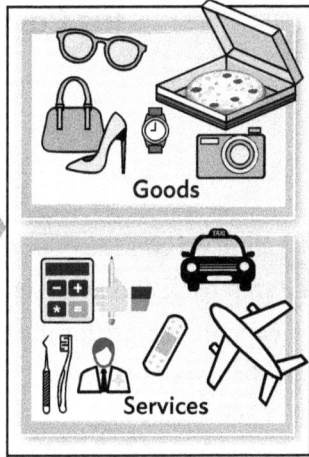

Labor

Capital

Goods

Services

The Power of Capital for the Common Person

Before we continue our investigation of production, let's step back and get a sense of proportion for the power of capital, not just for the billionaire industrialist but also for the common person.

Capitalism and the dramatic increase in the capital that people have access to have drastically improved our way of life. Take, for example, the food deliverers who use the app UberEats. These people have access to tremendous amounts of capital. What "capital" could I be talking about? Those delivery people are not bankers with millions of dollars to invest or large stock portfolios. They do not own factories or machines.

For a simple investment of $500 for a bicycle, $500 for a smartphone, and another $60 a month for a payment plan that allows the delivery person to connect to lightning-fast Internet and to the rest of the world, the UberEats delivery person has enough capital in hand to generate value that is roughly 10% to 70% more than the federal minimum wage[21]—something that the average bicycle rider would not have been able to do in the 1900s.

What has changed since the 1900s? The labor is still the same. A bike rider in the 1900s is not much different from a bike rider today. The streets he bikes on are very similar, just some asphalt and tar. The difference is the smartphone. Modern society is extraordinarily efficient at producing capital goods, such as access to the Internet, computational devices with tremendous processing power, and applications that can connect delivery people to hungry clients in seconds for a lump-sum cost of less than $1,000 and a recurring cost of $60 a month. This is equivalent to roughly 150 hours of a $7/hour job, which can include waiting tables, cleaning dishes, and stocking shelves. Stated in other words, the **cost** of producing unlimited Internet to access data stored in all corners of the globe and the **cost** of a mini-computer are **equivalent** to the value produced by a dishwasher at a restaurant working there for just a couple of weeks. That is truly amazing.

Here's another example to put into perspective how efficient we are at producing capital goods. One of the earliest broadly marketed computers was the IBM 360. This computer was the size of a room and had only a minute fraction of the computation power compared to the modern smartphone. It also did not have Internet access. That machine would have cost $2 million in today's (2020) money—far more than any average delivery person can afford.[22]

The size of the food-delivery market is estimated to be $26.5 billion.[23] A whopping $26.5 billion of services can be produced every year (and the industry is still growing) because of the capital provided to delivery people in the form of smartphones and cleverly designed apps.

The productivity of someone who knows how to ride a bike was unlocked and unleashed by his access to this kind of capital. When a person's access to capital increases, his production increases tremendously.

$$\text{Production} \uparrow \uparrow \uparrow = f(\text{L}, \text{K} \uparrow \uparrow \uparrow)$$

We Are All Capitalists
The Role You Play

Anybody can be a millionaire if everyone can produce like a millionaire. If everyone had a factory to his name that cranked out thousands of iPhones or had a construction company that could build an office building in a day, he would be rich beyond his wildest dreams. Access to capital is the key to wealth and productivity in the modern world. However, just like the goods and services we seek to consume, capital—the lifeblood of the modern world—is not infinite and comes from somewhere.

Capital, like any goods or services, needs to be made. We must produce capital just as we produce everything else. In our complex society today, *everyone* produces capital that powers the machines and the engines of the world. Many just don't know it.

Whether you are a lover of the free markets or a communist trying to bring down the system, we are all capitalists. We all use capital to produce, and we all consume the goods and services that are a result of our labor mixed with huge amounts of capital.

But where does capital come from? It comes from me and you, and from anybody who has access to a savings account. It's actually quite simple. Anything that you do not spend today is capital.

But isn't capital money that is spent on producing? How do dollars in a savings account help with production? After all, if you're like most people, with only a modest amount of savings, you are not scoping out large plots of land to find a good place to build your factory. Your reasons for saving could be to buy a house, a new car, to start a company, and so on. Regardless of your reasons, the bank takes those savings and lends it to businesses and entrepreneurs, who use these savings to build and maintain the machines and factories that make the goods and services today. Your savings account is, in essence, a small drop of gas in the economic engine that runs the world today—it may be as small as one screw on a plane engine—but it certainly isn't insignificant. Your savings come around to you the next time you fly to visit your loved ones. The plane that transports you may have a screw that was funded by your savings!

Tying Spending, Savings, Consumption, and Capital Together

Our first simple economic model is starting to connect disparate ideas—ideas that you are more familiar with—to how the world works.

Consumption is your spending, capital is your savings, and production is your earnings. Consumption is limited to your production, because consumption plus your savings is the total amount of production or earnings you have!

This means that all the goods and services that are produced fall into two categories; this gives us the following formula:

Production = Consumption (for today)
+ Capital (for tomorrow)

However, we know that

Production = f (Labor, Capital)

which means

$$\text{Production} = f(\text{Labor, Capital}) = \text{Spending (for today)} + \text{Savings (for tomorrow)}$$

What is the amount of capital you have today? It's the savings you've accumulated up to now! Substituting "spending" for consumption, "savings" for capital, and "earnings" for production

$$\text{Earnings} = f(\text{Labor, Savings up to now}) = \text{Spending (for today)} + \text{Savings (for tomorrow)}$$

INPUTS

Labor

Savings up to Now

OUTPUT/PRODUCTION

Goods

Service

=

EARNINGS

The statement above really isn't groundbreaking. Think about it from the perspective of your own spending and savings, as people are more familiar with their personal finances than details of the broader economy.

Every day, you spend money to live, and you save for tomorrow, based on what you make—your earnings. You cannot spend more than you make (without taking on debt), and you cannot save more than you make, either. The more you spend, the less you save. There is no reason that the economy as a whole would operate differently when there are millions of people doing what you are doing (spending, saving, and earning). The simple rules of personal finance apply also to the economy as a whole.

If you consume everything that you have produced today, not only will you compromise your ability to produce greater quantities in the future, you most likely will not be able to produce even the same amount as you did today. Capital goods, just like our bodies, suffer wear and tear from nature and must constantly be replenished.

An important part of our improved modern life is our ability to produce more goods and services than the minimum we need to consume to live. A person will be continuously stuck in grinding poverty if he eats everything that he grows today in order to survive. The ability to have a surplus and to save is something special that should not be taken for granted.

Why You Cannot Spend Your Way Out of Problems

Production = Spending + Savings

This formula has some very serious implications. If capital comes from savings, it is in direct competition with consumption, or spending.

This is the equation that shows why people trip up and focus so much on consumption (spending). They say that, if consumption and spending go up, production *must* go up. So why don't we just spend and spend and spend even if that requires borrowing money or printing money or taxing citizens? This doesn't work because spending does not do anything for our **ability to produce in the future**. In fact, it makes it worse. That is equivalent to saying that, if everyone eats bread, we will be able to produce more bread more efficiently for everyone, which is clearly non-sensical. The equation doesn't tell us the order in which things happen. It is clear that, in order for everyone to eat more bread, we must make more bread and not the other way around. The first logical fallacy is actually dangerous, because if we eat all the bread—including the seed corn that allows us to make bread tomorrow (our savings)—we are all going to starve tomorrow. We cannot spend or consume more than we produce. (Recall the There-Ain't-No-Such-Thing-as-a-Free-Lunch Law of Nature.)

Why would something that's not good for an individual ever be good for a group of individuals? No financial adviser would ever tell you to spend your way out of poverty. Why would it be different for the economy as a whole? Just as any annoying-but-wise person would tell you, you save your way to prosperity.

The only way you can consume more than you produce today is by consuming savings. The only way someone can consume more than he or she has produced or saved is by consuming someone else's savings. Any system that seeks to redistribute wealth is essentially breaching property rights by consuming other people's savings and surplus that they're saving for a rainy day. This is not only ethically wrong, based on our Free-Market Moral System, but myopic, because they are eating the capital that allows us to produce in abundance for tomorrow. If you are spending more than you are making, you are borrowing from the future by consuming today's surplus. You can continue to do this temporarily, while supplies last, but sooner or later, your surplus reserves will be gone.

How Do We Escape Poverty?

Consider this scenario:

Production = Spending

A society (or a person) stuck with this formula is in a pickle. There is no way that this society will ever escape poverty. If all production is used for basic sustenance, this society cannot save to invest in its future to produce more.

If all you ever do every day is spend twenty hours a day working on a farm or foraging to grow enough food for you to survive the night (which most people had to do before the Industrial Revolution and the rise of capitalism), you will never be able to escape this cycle. You'll never be able to play with your kids, learn how to play the guitar, or watch a play. There wouldn't be any actors, since aspiring thespians would also be stuck in the fields, lest they starve to death. More importantly, there would be no time to pick up an important skill, such as metalworking, to build the tools that would free up time from the farm in the first place.

The first step to accumulating capital is to produce enough to save via other means. There is only one other input we haven't considered: **labor**. The only way for a society (or person) to escape poverty and to begin to accumulate capital in the first place is to learn enough skills to improve its labor to produce enough to start saving. Then that person can start accumulating capital.

Computer Science Topic #8
The Deadly Exponential Function

Before we continue, we will use a short aside to introduce another important computer-science (or mathematical) concept. The speeds at which mathematical functions grow as their inputs go up are classified differently in computer science. The one function that all computer scientists are deathly afraid of is the **exponential function**. This means that the growth rate is proportional to the size of the amount present. Many things in nature follow exponential functions, such as cell division and population growth.

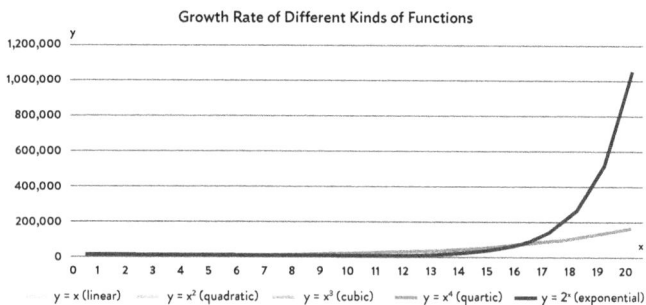

Growth Rate of Different Kinds of Functions

y = x (linear)   y = x² (quadratic)   y = x³ (cubic)   y = x⁴ (quartic)   y = 2ˣ (exponential)

Notice we can't even see the linear, quadratic, and cubic functions using this chart because the exponential function grows so quickly. To give a sense where the other functions are—at x = 20, the linear function's value is 20, the quadratic's is 400, the cubic's is 8,000, the quartic's 160,000, the exponential's is 1,048,576.

84

There are certain problems in life that we want to solve, but nobody has been able to show solutions that take less than exponential time. For example, you would be surprised that a rather trivial problem of, given "n," the number of packages, and fitting them into a truck in the most optimal manner possible doesn't have a clever solution other than trying every single possible arrangement. This is a huge problem, because even the most powerful computers in the world can't handle the number of possible solutions we have to test. For example, very simply, we'd have at least 3.6 million ways to arrange 10 packages in a straight line. It's much bigger if we consider three dimensions. A computer could test 3.6 million solutions in a reasonable amount of time, but if we had to find a solution for packing 100 packages in a truck (problems Amazon and UPS face every day), the possible solutions would be more than 9.33×10^{157}, which no super-computer could solve until the people reading this book and their great-, great-, great-grandchildren are dead. (If you are curious how businesses handle these problems, they essentially use solutions that approximate the optimal solution but are not 100% optimal, which take much less time to calculate but are not 100% efficient.)

While exponential functions are the bane of computer scientists, bankers and your savings account love exponential functions. You will be happy to learn that the interest that you earn behaves exponentially. That is something all capitalists (including you and me) benefit from every day.

A Silver Lining
The Power of Capital

I t isn't a coincidence that, since the Industrial Revolution—
or the "rise of capitalism"—that began in the 18th century,
the percentage of people living in extreme poverty dropped
from 90% to roughly 10% in less than 200 years.[24] Labor
and capital, both crucial inputs, do not behave in the same
way. People noticed that, since the Industrial Revolution,
a person's output is tied more to the amount of *capital* he
has rather than the amount of *labor* he puts in.

This certainly was not the case before the Industrial
Revolution. The output of someone's farm was basi-
cally determined by how much land he owned and
how many laborers he could get to work on his land.
The addition of an extra laborer did not dramatically
increase the farm's ability to produce. What this means
is that the input of labor behaves more like a linear
function. If you double the hours you spend working,
you get roughly twice the amount. Human beings were

stuck with no real way to dramatically improve their lives, their well-being bound by how many hours their bodies could handle in the fields. Another big problem was that, if increasing labor was the only means of producing more, more labor meant more mouths to feed! This means that, on average, the well-being of the average person was not increasing. If you're interested in learning more about this, please Google the *Malthusian Model.*

World Population Living in Extreme Poverty (1820-2015)[24]

Extreme poverty is defined as living on less than 1.90 international-$ per day.
International-$ are adjusted for price differences between countries and for price changes over time (inflation).

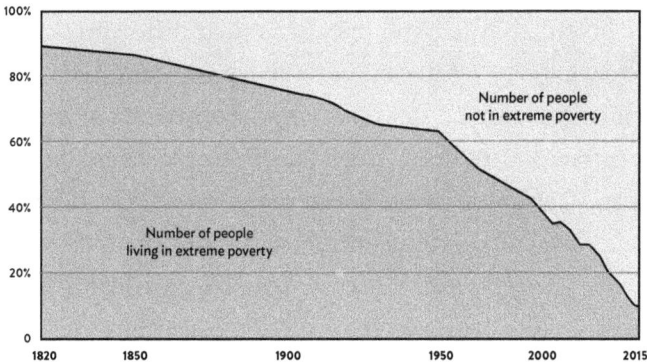

When the Industrial Revolution took place, new innovations such as the steam engine allowed people to multiply their output many, many times over, far more than labor ever could. The focus shifted from better labor to better capital. Imagine the number of horse carts it would take to haul a one-hundred car, steam-powered trainload from one end of America to the other.

World Population Living in Extreme Poverty (1820-2015)[24]

Extreme poverty is defined as living on less than 1.90 international-$ per day.
International-$ are adjusted for price differences between countries and for price changes over time (inflation).

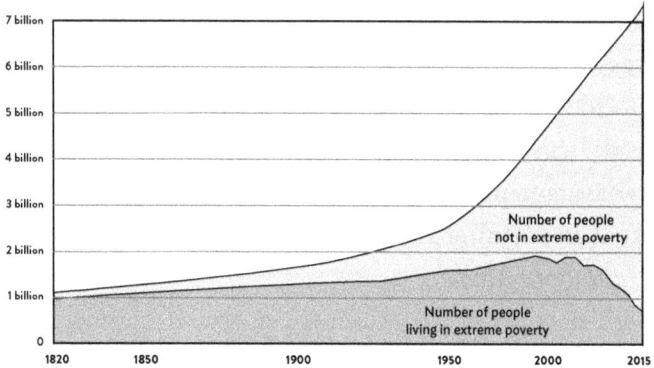

Fortunately, capital operates much differently from labor. Labor does not beget more labor. Working longer hours in farmland does not lengthen an hour, nor does it miraculously double the number of workers on the farm. Capital, however, begets capital. Someone who owns a factory can use the profits from the factory to create a new factory. His profits are increased from both factories, which allows him to build even more factories at a faster pace. The growth of capital—and therefore of output—behaves more like an exponential function, increasing at a faster rate every day. Thus, the average output per person can increase exponentially as well, meaning the average well-being of the person can also increase extremely quickly.

People have used this exponential-growth mechanism of capital to climb out of poverty at staggering rates. From

1981 to 2013, the fraction of the Earth's population living on less than a dollar a day has dropped from more than 40% to only 14%.[25] Once you get the ball rolling, with people accumulating capital, wealth can grow extremely quickly.

What applies to the economy as a whole applies to your personal finances, too. Consider this example: You are a janitor, and you earn $10 an hour. Ignoring the effects of taxes, this translates to roughly $24,000 a year. If you worked 40 years before retiring, your total earnings would be $960,000. However, if you saved money in your savings account (in other words, if you accumulate capital), you would earn interest. Then, the next year, you would earn interest on that interest (capital begets capital). If you started off with $136,363 and saved that sum at 5% a year, you would make the same amount—$960,000—by the time you retire. The slightest difference in how much you can grow your capital drastically changes the math, since it's an exponential function. If you managed to grow your capital by 8% every year, you would need to start off with only $44,190. If you managed to grow your capital by 10%, you would need only $21,211, without working a day in your life! Just as your parents tell you from day one, you *save your way to prosperity*. In other words, to become better off, you need to grow your capital.

The power of capital can be seen in the wealthy today. To be wealthy before the Industrial Revolution, you had to be a king or duke to take away, in the form of taxes, from other people in order to amass wealth. Today, the majority of the mega-wealthy are not nobility but rather business owners or, in other words, owners of capital. Very few of the wealthy today become wealthy through salaries or labor alone. Business owners themselves do not have high salaries. Warren Buffett, who has a net worth of more than $80 billion,[26] gets paid a salary of $100,000 a year.[27] The CEO of Goldman Sachs, one of the most profitable investment banks in the world, has a salary of $28 million a year.[28] Relying on this salary alone, it would take the CEO more than 2,850 years to amass the wealth of Buffett.

Business owners become rich simply because they are, in essence, better savers and accumulators of capital. They do more with their savings, or capital, which allows them

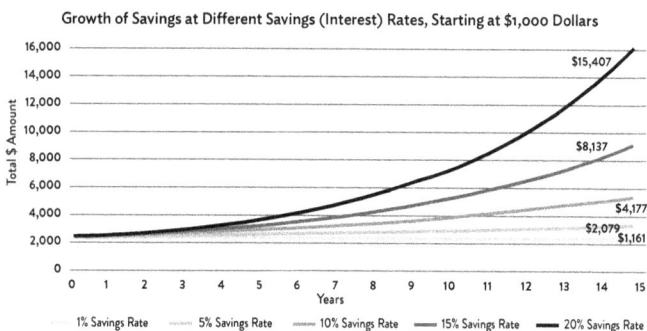

Growth of Savings at Different Savings (Interest) Rates, Starting at $1,000 Dollars

Savings Rate (Interest Rate)/Year	Starting Money to Make $1 Million Dollars After 40 Years
1%	$671,653.14
2%	$452,890.42
5%	$142,045.68
8%	$46,030.93
10%	$22,094.93
15%	$3,733.24
20%	$680.38

to compound their savings better than most people. The primary mechanism by which they grow their savings, rather than putting it in a savings account, is by investing their savings in a business. The business they invest in typically is a business they built themselves. In other words, the business ends up being their piggy bank rather than a Wells Fargo savings account. Any profits or interest they make off that business, they put back into the business to grow. The only difference is that the business grows much faster than the interest of a Wells Fargo savings account.

Warren Buffett has made, on average, roughly 20% a year on his "savings."[29] If you had just started off with $50,000, and you grew your savings by 20% for 40 years, you would retire with $73 million—which is equivalent to a salary of $1.8 million every year, a salary not even Buffett has.

Labor doesn't grow labor, but capital begets capital. That, quite simply, is the power of capital.

The Fundamental Solution Restated

Now that we know more about capital and labor, we can restate the fundamental solution. The fundamental problem is that we need to consume. The fundamental solution, originally, was to produce. However, we know that the way people produce these days is primarily through capital. The real "fundamental solution" is to accumulate and maintain capital, which is the means of production.

The Real Question

Understanding how goods and services are produced, we now know that the question is not "How can we provide people with livable wages?" Rather, it is "How can we make people more productive, in order to improve their standards of living, by ensuring they can accumulate the capital they need?"

Over the course of history, there really have been only three ways to do it. The laws of nature do not make capital free, and it has to come from somewhere.

- You can work for it. If you are not fortunate enough to be born with it, you'll need to earn it. Fortunately, in the modern economy, skilled labor to operate capital is well-rewarded. Skilled metal workers, technicians, programmers, and managers all command salaries well above the minimum to maintain a healthy life. Most people who do not inherit millions or billions from their families will have to go through this. This is why we have the common message from our moms and dads urging us to work hard at school, not to skip class, to do our homework, and to graduate from a good college. These are mechanisms to sharpen our skills and to increase the output of labor. When people's productivity of labor increases, they will be able to start accumulating capital of their own.

- You can inherit it. If you are fortunate to inherit your wealth, you really don't need to do much except preserve your capital, which is easier said than done. We've heard the common adage "From shirtsleeves to shirtsleeves in three generations." It's so well-known that, even on the other side of the world, the Chinese have the exact same saying: "Prosperity does not last for more than three generations." Capital is extremely difficult to accumulate but easily squandered.

- You can steal it. By fraud or at gunpoint, you can take away someone's hard-earned savings illegally, or legally via wealth transfers, taxation, and confiscations. Typically, governments are the best at misappropriating wealth. Consider North Korea's dictator, who has wealth estimated at $5 billion[30], while most of the country he runs does not have access to electricity.

Injection of Ethics Into Our
Economic System

Now that we have a basic economic model created, let's try to fit in ethics. How do the moral theorems we discussed earlier come into play? We showed earlier that our Free-Market Moral System was able to prove, from our starting Axioms, the Creator-Is-the-Owner and the Stealing-Is-Bad Theorems. This is, in essence, a moral system that defends property rights. Stated in our new economic language—**it is a defense of people's savings**, which they have earned through blood, sweat, and tears—or even through luck. A defense of savings is a defense of property. A defense of property is a defense against any form of systematic stealing or slavery. A defense against stealing and slavery is a defense of life and the belief that life is sacred.

You can't be free if you can't keep what you've earned. Tyranny starts with the confiscation of property before it becomes a full-blown attack on human life and well-being. If you control the means of production, or capital, you control the lives of people. Milton Friedman stated very accurately that a free market is a necessary condition of a free society.[31]

In a free society, the **only way to get a surplus is to provide a product or service that someone else values** (recall the Voluntary-Trade Theorem). Therefore, the only way to morally change one person's surplus for another is through voluntary trade! Most social programs that claim to help someone are fundamentally transfers of wealth that consume another person's savings, and, in our ethical system, that is no different from stealing or, in drastic cases, systematic slavery.

We stated earlier in this book that, too much of the time, proponents of liberty try to argue using statistics or facts to prove that certain policies are effective. There are debates on how much to tax and how much to spend on this social program versus another. Most of the time, I find that such exercises are futile. Statistics are cherry-picked to make certain policies seem more effective, and the second- and third-order effects are usually difficult to calculate. Most people fail to address what I believe to be more important. Is such an action moral? Are the solutions being proposed ethical, or are they a means of stealing from one person to give to another, regardless of the intentions?

This is precisely why we need not only to lean on a mental economic model, but we must also have a rigorous, consistent, and thought-out ethical model. Neither of these systems can exist in a vacuum. Economic and natural limitations guide us in what we believe to be fair or right. What we believe to be fair or right should drive how we interact with our fellow humans.

PART III

OUR MODEL IN ACTION

Now that we have an ethical and economic model we can use to think about the world, let's see the application of these two combined in a myriad of situations.

The world has become so complex that people may have forgotten the steps required to consume. To make things much simpler, we will use as an example a small town, named Cornville. In this town, the only thing people eat to survive is corn, and the only thing they make is corn. Imagine corn as a representation of all the goods and services we consume today. Surplus corn not eaten on the day of production is saved, either for the day after or as the seeds for next season's crop.

Farmer Joe in Grinding and Abject Poverty

F armer Joe is an upstanding citizen of Cornville. He works hard every day on his ten-acre farm and plants corn like all the other citizens of Cornville. He tills his own land with his hoe and sows the corn seed himself. He walks through the fields every day and waters the crops with his trusty watering can. It is back-breaking work. And for all the effort he puts in, he is able to produce only three full corncobs every day.

At the end of each day, however, he gets hungry, and he needs to eat, or **consume**, three cobs, one each for breakfast, lunch, and dinner, in order to survive. He still ends up pretty hungry at the end of the day, but he is fortunate that three is enough to sustain him and give him strength to work the next day. However, he ends up no better off than when he started the day. He becomes extremely frustrated because, after all his work, his life is not improving. He is unable to accumulate any wealth, or **surplus**.

One day, Farmer Joe sits on the floor of his little shack, and he starts to wonder why he can't produce more. He certainly works hard and puts in the time and effort. He is strong and can work without taking many breaks. He realizes that he is putting a significant amount of **labor** into producing corn. However, he also realizes that the tools he has are not good enough. Plowing by himself is too slow, and his watering can is too unwieldy. He surmises that, if he can get his hands on better tools, or **capital**, he will be able to make more corn!

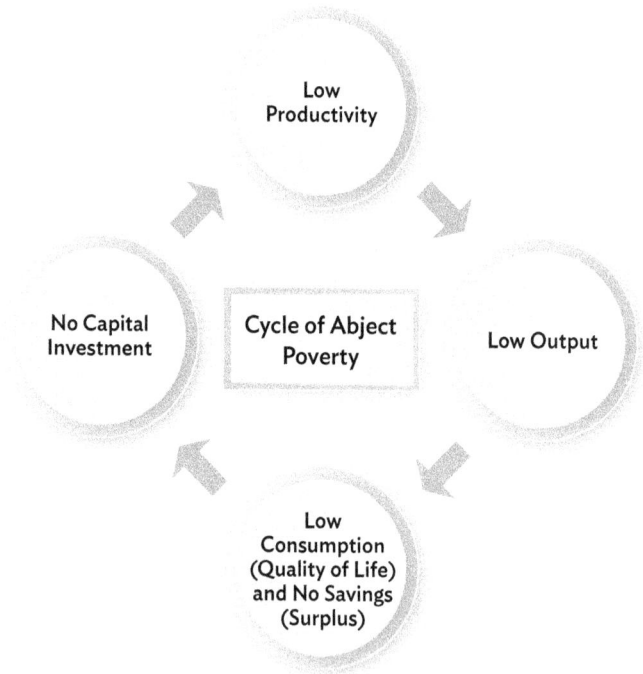

Low
Productivity

No Capital
Investment

Cycle of Abject
Poverty

Low Output

Low
Consumption
(Quality of Life)
and No Savings
(Surplus)

A faraway merchant, Merchant Zheng, comes to Cornville every day, offering rare and exotic wares from distant lands. This merchant has something called a "tractor"—a metal mechanical beast that makes terrifying noises but can carry hundreds of pounds of seed corn and watering cans. This merchant is willing to trade this tractor for a hundred cobs of corn.

Farmer Joe realizes that, if he is able to get his hands on this tractor, his quality of life will improve significantly. He will be able to eat more corn and be happier. He realizes the predicament he is in. Because he is unable to make more than he eats every day, he will never be able to save any corn or have any **savings**. Because he is never able to save any corn, he cannot get the tools he needs to make more corn and accumulate **savings**. He is stuck in an infinite loop of **abject poverty**.

Joe's Angels and Demons
An Ethical Dilemma

F armer Joe thinks that this situation is surely unfair, and, in his helplessness, he starts to think about ways to steal the merchant's tractor. He thinks he is justified in this. After all, he **needs** it more than the merchant! The merchant must have mountains of corn in his granary if he is able to sell tractors to everybody. Surely, stealing just one tractor won't do any harm. Joe is resolute. Tomorrow, he will walk up to the merchant, wrestle him to the ground, and take the tractor from him. He sleeps soundly.

Farmer Joe wakes up with a calm mind. He starts to question the decision he made last night. First, he wonders about the consequences of his actions. The king of Cornville hates stealing. The king's fundamental beliefs, or **axioms**, lead him to conclude that any form of **hurting others is wrong**. From his axioms, he concludes logically that stealing is a form of hurting others. The king **forbids** any form of stealing and threatens to execute robbers and thieves who do not abide by his laws.

However, Farmer Joe is not satisfied with just obeying laws. He wants to know *why* the king has come to these conclusions. Farmer Joe agrees that hurting others is wrong, and he can see clearly why stealing hurts people. Farmer Joe realizes, however, that, despite the fact that he is bigger and stronger than Merchant Zheng, stealing from Zheng will have terrible implications. He knows that his neighbor, Farmer Bob, used to be a heavyweight boxing champion and could easily overpower him. Joe thinks to himself, *If I steal from Zheng because I think I need to, what is stopping Bob from stealing from me? After all, Bob has children and surely also needs corn to feed his hungry children.* Therefore, he concludes that stealing from Merchant Zheng is **immoral**, and he decides not to do it.

At the same time, he realizes that his jealousy and hatred for Merchant Zheng is unfounded. He now knows that, since the king strictly forbids Merchant Zheng from stealing, Merchant Zheng must have managed to save enough corn himself before he had his first tractor. After all, the tractor must have come from someone. Even if Merchant Zheng stole the tractor from another person, someone must have made that tractor, using his profits from surplus corn **in the first place**. You can't steal a tractor before it was ever made!

Therefore, someone out there was able to produce enough corn without the first tractor—perhaps it was Merchant Zheng. Joe, instead of stealing from Zheng, decides to ask for his advice. One day, he walks up to

Merchant Zheng and asks him, "How did you manage to make enough corn before you got your first tractor?" Merchant Zheng replies, "That, my friend, is a secret I wish to keep to myself. It took me two years to figure out, and, therefore, I do not wish to give this advice for free. But I will give you some hope that it is certainly possible. You just need to be cleverer with what you have."

Joe is frustrated, but he now realizes that Merchant Zheng's response is perfectly fair. He is not allowed to steal **goods**, such as the tractor, but he is also not allowed to force **service** out of someone. After all, if Joe took ten years to figure out how to make more corn by being cleverer, he wouldn't want other people to steal his secrets for free. He would not want to be working for someone for free or to be another person's **slave**.

The Great Escape

After two years of struggle, Farmer Joe realizes, through his experience and wisdom gained on the job, that, if he buries the empty corncobs, the nutrients go back into the earth, and the corn he plants grows faster. He is now a more-skilled and wiser farmer. Joe has more **human capital**. In other words, he has become better at **labor**, effectively increasing the output of his **labor**. He is now able to make four corncobs a day. Finally, he is productive enough to have a **surplus**, and he begins to **save**.

After 100 days of back-breaking work, Joe is extremely excited. He walks up to Merchant Zheng with a bag of 100 corncobs and gets a shiny tractor. Both Merchant Zheng and Joe are happy, because they are now both **better off** with this **voluntary trade**. Joe goes back home and with his tractor and realizes that the tractor is super useful. It allows him to produce 100 corncobs a day! **The effect of capital was much more than the effect of his labor!**

Joe's life is better off in numerous ways. He doesn't need to lug around a heavy watering can anymore, and he can eat much more corn so that he's not hungry at the end of the day. He saves the rest of the corn as seed corn so he can grow more corn. He finds that his output is growing **exponentially**, since each day his larger crop provides him with more seed corn than the day before. He is now benefiting from the **compounding effects of capital**. He has managed to escape the abject poverty he once lived in by becoming much more **productive** and is on his way to becoming **wealthy**.

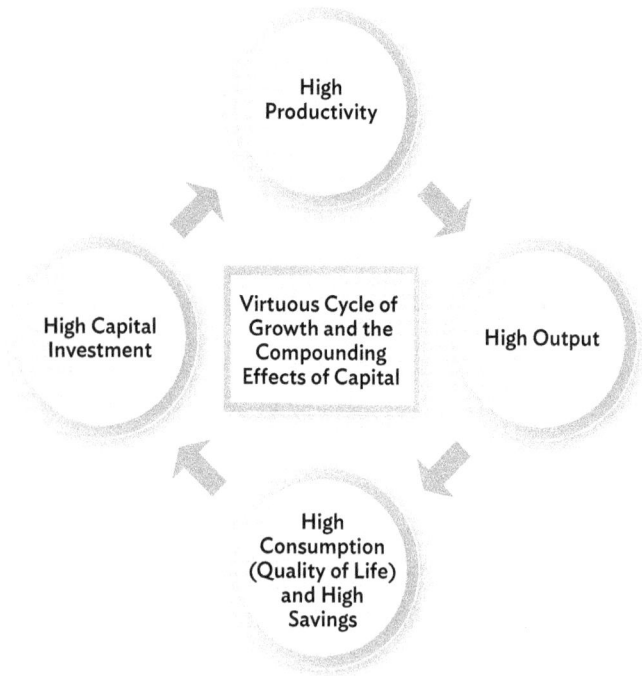

Meet Farmer Bob

Now that Farmer Joe is fairly well off and producing hundreds of corncobs a day, he decides to get married and have kids. To spend more time with his family, he hires his neighbor Bob to use his farm, tractor, and seed corn to manage the farm and to grow crops for him. To entice Bob to leave his farm, which produces only three cobs a day, Joe offers to pay him six cobs a day. Bob accepts.

Bob uses the tractor to plant the seeds and water Joe's crops. It is tiring work. Joe, on the other hand, lounges around and plays with his kids every day. Bob becomes resentful. He thinks to himself, *This is not fair. I'm doing all the work and getting paid only six cobs a day, but Joe is the one who's making hundreds of corncobs a day off of my labor!*

Bob decides that, tomorrow, he will use his superior strength and boxing skills to take over Joe's farm, or, at the very least, force Joe to pay him more! Surely ten cobs a day will do little to affect Joe's overall wealth. Overnight, however, Bob thinks to himself, *If I forcefully take over Joe's Farm, not only will the king punish me, but I know that*

Sally, next door, used to be in Special Forces military. What's to stop Sally from taking over the farm the next day? Then, I'll be left with nothing—except for my life, if I'm lucky. **Force**, he realizes, is not the answer. Perhaps negotiation is a better method. He can threaten to quit working for Joe for anything less than seven cobs a day. However, he also knows that Sally is willing to do the same work, or **compete** with Bob for the job. She's willing to do the work for only six cobs a day. Bob realizes then that he has no **negotiating leverage**. What about his pride? Surely, he won't stand for this little bit of pay. Maybe he'll quit regardless! What are his alternatives then? He could go back to his own corn farm that has no tractor and do even harder work for only three cobs a day. Bob thinks that's a terrible idea.

Bob comes to the sudden realization that he's actually quite lucky. His **best option** is to work for Joe. No one is compelling him to stay at Joe's farm, and if there were a better option out there, no one could stop him from taking it. He's making twice the amount he used to make on his old farm, and the only reason for that is that he is **able to use Joe's tractor, or capital**, which Bob knows **Joe worked hard to save for**. Bob thinks to himself that when he does get a tractor himself, he does not want Sally to be able to take it from him whenever she wants. Bob decides to continue to work hard on Joe's farm.

The Great Escape
Part II

ob continues to work on Joe's farm with the tractor. He slowly becomes more skillful at using it and actually becomes better at running a farm than Joe had ever been. The output of his **labor** has improved drastically, and he has now doubled the output of Joe's farm. Joe's competitor offers to hire Bob at twelve corn cobs a day—twice the amount Joe is paying him. But Joe, realizing Bob's new skills are easily worth more than twelve cobs a day, counters by offering Bob twenty-four corncobs per day, which Bob happily accepts. Bob realized that, even though Sally was still willing to work on Joe's farm for fewer corncobs than Bob would, Sally cannot match Bob's experience and skill. Therefore, Bob realizes greater rewards for his work. Even though Bob does not own the capital and tractor Joe has, Bob is making a much-better living for himself by being a skilled user of that capital. He is now able to save and to accumulate capital himself.

Bob joins Joe in escaping from abject poverty and makes a better life for himself. Bob did it by improving his labor output. Joe did it by accumulating capital.

PART IV

ADVANCED TOPICS AND COMMON MISCONCEPTIONS

We can already see that, in our story of Joe the Farmer, we have already begun to address some issues that we have not discussed. This part will investigate some of those more-advanced topics that we can add to enrich our economic model as well as address some common economic misconceptions that people have that hinder people's ability to accumulate capital and to make themselves better off. We will do so through both an economic and ethical lens.

The Force of Nature vs.
the Force of Man

Many people confuse the difference between the force of nature and the force of man, which leads to some dangerous conclusions. Forces of nature are the laws of nature that govern all life, from the lion prides of the Serengeti to the angler fish down in the Mariana Trench. Forces of nature cannot be reasoned with. You cannot protest against hunger or famine and magically cause a tree to bear fruit, nor can you pass a law that makes it illegal for a dry well not to provide us with water.

The force of man, however, is something we can prohibit. Laws, studies of ethics, and government institutions are weapons of the common man for facing off against thugs, thieves, and bandits. The force of man is what we believe wholeheartedly to be unethical and is the underpinning of not only our simple ethical framework but of most of Western civilization. It is what allows us to readily condemn the Gestapo and the Kremlin, and it is also what causes us to look in disgust at the atrocities that happened at Auschwitz.

However, there are instances in which people confuse the force of nature with the force of man. Take, for instance, in times of drought, the person with a well who charges triple what he normally charges for water. Many people would condemn this person for being unethical, and, while I also frown upon such price-gouging in times of need, such action *cannot*—in our ethical framework—be considered unethical. **A price is merely a suggestion**, and if a person does not want the water, he or she is free to walk away. Just because negotiating power is in the hands of the producer does not mean he is condemning people to die from thirst. If the producer were not there providing water with his well, **there would be no water for sale in the first place**. If he lowers his price, **there would not be enough water for everyone at that price** (we will take a **look at price ceilings later on**). We cannot morally force this person to part ways with his water at a price he does not want to. **There is no difference between forcing him to sell at a lower price and stealing a portion of his water to give to those who are thirsty**. At the end of the day, if you don't like the price that he is charging for water, don't buy it. Your needs may include water, but that does not mean you can compel someone to supply your needs.

The key thing to understand is that, while the circumstances above are terrible places to be in, to morally condemn this person opens up a train of thought that leads to inconsistency, similar to what we established in our discussion of socialist attempts at expanding our ethical framework, which justifies all kinds of stealing and unethical behavior. Ethical models can prohibit only the force of man; they can do nothing against the force of nature.

Price Controls on Necessities

People need to bolster their economic models with a better grasp of the concept of price. As regular, everyday consumers, most people do not see the price mechanism from a producer's point of view. They walk into a grocery store, and they either accept the price or move on to the next product, thinking that they have no effect or say on the price of products. Some even believe that prices are what corporations force upon helpless victims to extract every penny from them. They point to necessities such as lifesaving surgeries, water, food, and medicines. When they see the high price tag on these goods and services, they become upset.

In our economic model, we need to have a better understanding of what prices are. A price is merely an indication of the level at which a transaction could possibly take place. A price in a competitive marketplace, in which there are multiple providers of a good or service, is the best approximation for the **clearing** price of that particular good or service. It also is a good approximation of the **economic cost** of a good or service. This essentially means that the profits from providing this good or service are just enough so that the producer is not going to give up producing this good for a better opportunity out there.

The **law of supply and demand** for a good or service assumes two pretty obvious things: as prices go down, more people want it (and more people can afford to buy it). As price goes up, more people want to make it (or can afford to make it).

Many people see grocery stores full of food, and they think that the only reason that it costs a certain amount is so that a firm can make a big, fat profit, as if there's an endless supply of food that the store could sell at that price and that customers could either take it or leave it. That could not be further from the truth. The reason that prices for goods that are produced in competition with others are set that way is that these are the prices in which the amount they are willing and **able to produce at that price** matches the number of people who want to buy it. There is very little the producer can do to change this price and to deviate from this price.

In highly competitive environments, the profit a store can make gets squeezed to almost nothing, even in industries that people think are exorbitantly expensive, such as health insurance. Most insurance companies have a profit margin (the number of cents they make per dollar of revenue) of only 2-3%![32] Even restaurants typically have a higher margin than that, at roughly 6%![33]

In a freely competitive environment, prices are the lowest that firms can possibly charge in order to continue to do business and provide those goods and services at that quantity. Otherwise, people who see firms making such high profits will be incentivized to start their own businesses and compete for those abnormally high profits. This means that, for the vast majority of goods and services that the regular consumer buys, the bargaining power is in the hands of the consumer.

With this in mind, consider the most direct method of trying to help someone out—price controls. Many believe that goods deemed necessary for life, such as food, basic housing, and healthcare should have price controls. But what people fail to understand is that the prices in a free market are already the lowest they can possibly be in order to provide the amounts we are used to seeing. Implementing price controls is the same as treating symptoms for a disease. The real problem people should address is that the economic cost of producing something is too high. The symptoms of high costs are the high prices that the consumer sees. Time and time again, ancient Romans realized that the more price controls you put on food, the more starvation and famine you will have.

If you limit the price of important medication, which, in this example, costs $80 a pill, to $40 a pill, you are not helping those who can't afford the medication at the higher price. Since the prices are artificially low, producers are not willing to produce or able to produce (due to costs) as much of the drug. On the other hand, more people are willing or able to buy the drug at the lower price. This means you will have a shortage of the drug, and rationing must occur. There will still be people (in this case, more people) who want the drug but can't get their hands on it. Instead of the price being the mechanism for determining who gets the drug, it'll be the person rationing the drug who decides. This person could be some unelected bureaucrat who gets a fee for doing the rationing. Notice that, absent price controls, the amount available of that drug is greater than the amount in an environment where price controls occur. The best (and only moral) way to help people in need is to create an environment that allows people to be more productive, efficient, and competitive. The more productive a drug-maker and its suppliers are, the lower the economic cost of creating the important drug. That way, more people will be able to afford it. More importantly, more people will be able to consume it because the producer can produce more and at lower prices more efficiently.

Another good way of understanding why price controls do not work is to consider an extreme case. Instead of reducing the price of the drug to $40, why don't we just make it $0? People will say it is impossible, since the firm cannot make a profit and will go out of business. They are correct, but what they fail to understand is that, if the drug is at $80, there usually is no large cushion of profit between that price and $0. Most likely, the economic cost-per-unit of producing that drug at those quantities is $80. The firm becomes economically unprofitable even at *$79*, in this case.

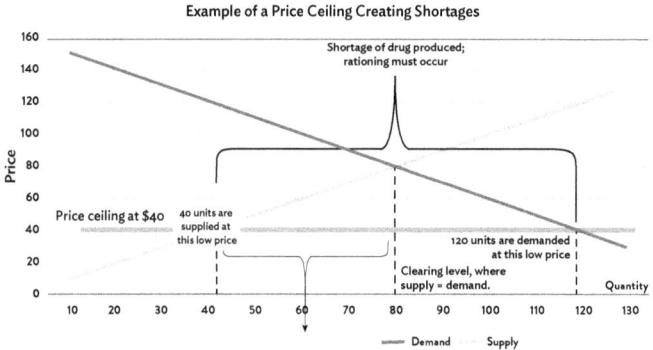

Example of a Price Ceiling Creating Shortages

Without a price ceiling, more of the drug would have been produced, and no rationing is needed

Direct Government Provision
of Necessities

Many people believe that governments should provide necessities. However, with our newfound knowledge, we can immediately see why this does not work. In a competitive environment, firms will produce the quantity of necessities required at the lowest possible price, as evidenced by the low profit margins of most industries. Why do people believe that an organization such as the government, which does not need to compete and fight every day in order to survive and remain in business, will be able to produce the goods more efficiently? Does the government have better technology or human resources at a cheaper price than private firms? Most, if not all, of the time, government production of goods is much more costly than private production.

Misunderstanding the Magic Formula
What Is and Isn't a Zero-Sum Game

Taking another look at our magical formula,

Production = Consumption + Capital

We learned earlier that this formula applies to the economy as a whole as well as to individuals. Another way of expressing the above is

Earnings = Spending + Savings

We've discussed earlier in the book how people often can make faulty logical claims based on the equation above. The equation states several obvious relationships: you cannot consume more than you produce or have saved up until now, and you cannot spend more than you earn (unless you borrow, which is essentially consuming from someone else's savings and promising to pay them back). It does not, however, tell us the relationship of what comes first. To reiterate, production comes first; consumption and capital follow. Earnings come first; spending and savings follow.

The first fallacy we addressed is that, if people consume more, then production must increase. It was clear how that made very little sense. That's equivalent to saying, "If we eat more, we automatically become more efficient farmers."

A second big fallacy people get caught up in is that people do not understand what is and what isn't a zero-sum game. They mistakenly believe that the money you earn is a zero-sum game. A zero-sum game means that if someone benefits, someone must suffer, because the sum of their earnings is a fixed number. A big misunderstanding is that if I earn a million dollars, this means that someone or a group of people must earn less by a total of a million dollars. When we focus on earnings or production, we can show in a simple example that this certainly isn't the case. If Farmer Bob is growing corn in Cornville, and Farmer Jenny is growing blueberries in Blueville, the fact that Farmer Bob grows more will not have any effect on Farmer Jenny's ability to grow more blueberries. If Farmer Bob grows more, he earns more. If Farmer Jenny grows more, she earns more. Both of them can improve their lives and their earnings by producing more. The overall size of the proverbial production pie increases, and everybody is better off. This is why people use the phrase "making money" or "earning money" as opposed to "being given money by your employer" or being "distributed money." Production creates value.

However, if we focus on the other side of the equation, namely, consumption, there are certain instances in which it *is* a zero-sum game. Redistribution of wealth (of current earnings and savings) is certainly a zero-sum game. Focusing on redistribution of produced goods, you can redistribute only the amount of goods and services we have produced today and have saved till now. While you can certainly redistribute future production, the act of redistribution says nothing about production tomorrow, and there is ample evidence that redistribution destroys future ability to produce. (The deaths associated with—and other disastrous effects of land redistribution in Zimbabwe and China—are discussed in more detail on page 150.) Therefore, when we look at redistribution, if someone gets more, then someone must get less.

Labor Is an Input to Production
and Is Not the Same as Ownership

One thing we saw in Cornville was that Bob was not happy that he was doing all the work on Joe's farm and that Joe was reaping most of the rewards from the farm. While it does seem unfair at first glance, people who have this view fail to understand the different inputs that are provided to the output of Joe's corn crop. Remember, there are **two inputs** to production, and nobody is getting any corn for free, even though, on the surface, it does seem like Joe has a cushy life. Bob is doing all the **work** or **labor**, but Joe provided all the **capital** or **savings**. Labor and capital are rewarded in their own ways. It just so happens that, in this environment, access to capital is much harder and more expensive than access to labor. These inputs are compensated in different ways. Labor is an input negotiated separately and is fairly paid to workers according to the clearing price of labor, also called **wages**. Providing the capital is ownership. After all expenses, including the expenses of labor, the owner keeps whatever profits are left over.

Bob figured this out when he realized three things: 1) Bob voluntarily agreed to take the job from Joe at an agreed-upon wage. Bob can quit anytime he wants to if he does not like the job or wage. 2) If Bob demanded to be paid more, he would have lost his job to Sally, who would have done the same work for the same amount or even less. Thus, Bob is paid fairly, no more and no less. 3) There is nothing stopping Bob from quitting and starting his own farm, except for the fact that Bob does not have the capital to buy a tractor and start working for himself on his own farm. Bob **cannot skip steps to accumulate capital without stealing** from Joe.

There may be a time in the future where our productivity increases to a point where capital is so cheap that labor can be rewarded more so than capital, but those days are far away.

More Spending (and Consumption)
Is Not Always Good
Chasing Dollars Rather Than Value

M any proponents of central planning or socialism get
hooked on the fact that higher spending per person
must mean that each person is better off. It doesn't matter
if the government is spending the money or if a private
citizen is spending the money; spending = good! First,
spending too much today destroys our ability for future
production and growth. Second, there is another fundamental misunderstanding that is taking place here—the
differentiation between production and currency.

Economists measure the gross output of people in dollars as a **proxy** for measuring well-being and production of
a person or nation. The true number that economists are
trying to figure out is the number of goods and services
we are producing: how many haircuts per year, how many
cab rides are given, how many strawberries are grown, and
so on. Goods and services are the things that improve the
quality of our lives—not dollar bills, which are, essentially,

fancy strips of paper. The challenge is: How much do we **value** a haircut? Is a haircut worth five strawberries or twenty-thousand? Similarly, with wages, we could easily be paid in strawberries. However, that will prove to be difficult in many ways. A strawberry might be much more valuable to a sweet-tooth like me than to someone who's deathly allergic to berries. We solve all these problems by introducing a medium, which we call "currency." We convert all our strawberries to dollars and our haircuts to dollars and add them up.

Naturally, we then ask, how many dollars is a haircut or a strawberry worth? Again, this is where individual **values** come into play. For a strawberry producer, the value of a strawberry is at least above a certain number, usually its **cost**. For a strawberry eater, a strawberry is how much he likes it and is willing to pay for it. If those two numbers work out, and the strawberry eater is willing to pay more than the price that the strawberry producer is willing to sell at, then a **voluntary transaction** will take place. The price of that strawberry transaction is precisely the value it has brought to society. If you value a strawberry at only $1 and the producer values it at $2, no transaction will take place, and, thus, no value is bestowed upon society. If we sum up all the dollars of all these transactions that take place, we now know the **value** in currency of all the goods and services produced!

Currency is a measurement of value but is not value in itself. If we have a bunch of sloths living in Slothland, each with a million dollars, lying around doing nothing, it would be absurd to say that those sloths are millionaires. What can they buy with the money? Nothing, as there are no goods and services produced in Slothland.

In a free society, **value is accurately captured by spending**, because nobody will spend or transact a trade if the good or service consumed does not give them at least that amount of value. However, in a controlled economy, this relationship between spending and value breaks down. Compare these two scenarios: Farmer Bob exchanges 10 tons of corn to Sally for $1,000. That's $1,000 of value realized, or this transaction would not take place. More importantly, in this scenario, 10 tons of corn was grown in that economy. If the government spends $1,000 to pay Slothy Sheridan to lie around and do nothing, the amount of currency spent in both scenarios is the same, but in the second scenario, there certainly wasn't $1,000 of product produced.

Capitalism Is a Big Value
Voting Machine

Governments don't have values. People have values. Strawberries don't mean anything to a government body. A government body does not enjoy the nutrition or taste of a strawberry. Individual consumers do.

The best way for values to be expressed collectively is through free markets and a free economy. Free markets are the ultimate voting machine. People vote for what is important to them by what they spend.

The amazing thing about the modern economy is this: **No one is telling anybody what to make!** There is no Commissar for Breadmaking or Bureau of Auto Manufacturing telling anybody to make a certain number of each good. Yet, every day of the year, we are never in want of bread or cars. The modern economy is able to produce everything that we could possibly want and need to survive. The transmission mechanism that signals the economy and its people, telling it exactly what to produce, is **prices**. This is why it is extraordinarily important to preserve prices in their most natural state, for it tells us—without any force involved—what is important. Any attempt to distort prices will cause overproduction and waste or a shortage. Free markets are a big voting machine, and people vote with their dollars by either accepting or rejecting prices.

Take, for example, baseball. America has voted with its citizens' wallets, and its people are willing to spend billions of dollars in total each year to watch baseball. We have gigantic baseball stadiums in many cities and baseball diamonds in every school, while there are very few baseball stadiums in the United Kingdom. Are massive stadiums such as PNC Park constructed through the powers of the federal government? Is the UK Parliament just biased against baseball? No, these multi-billion-dollar structures are constructed by private corporations because the people of America voted with their dollars that they value baseball more than their British peers do!

Government spending in areas that the free market can provide very likely leads to less value and more waste. If the UK Parliament spends tax money to build baseball stadiums that otherwise would not have been built by a free market, that means that the baseball stadium will be losing money in the long run. Otherwise, the free market would have built it.

Consider another, more-extreme example. I never fully understood the game of baseball. However, I am a huge fan of tennis. If I were King of America, you can be sure that every street corner would have not only a clay tennis court but also a hard court as well. If I'm feeling generous, I'll also throw in some very costly grass courts for good measure. While in my mind, the public value and welfare of America has increased, since I value tennis ten times more than I do baseball, I am actually making people worse off because most Americans like baseball more than they like tennis. By forcing my values upon other people, society as a whole loses. Free markets are perfect mechanisms for people to express their values in a fair and proportional manner with their money and spending.

Cronyism Is Not Capitalism

A rather sizable portion of people who dislike free markets find fault with capitalism because they believe that large corporations can spend a lot of money to lobby politicians for favors to benefit companies at the expense of the taxpayer or common citizen. This is true. But what people don't realize is that this "cronyism"—asking for special government favors—is not a byproduct of free markets but rather a byproduct of the common practice of government intervention.

In our Free-Market Axioms, it is clear that *any* kind of political favor (which involves forceful reallocation of resources) to *any* interest group is immoral. This includes favors for businesses. The problem is that most socialists who try to push their agenda through the government and political powers-that-be use the very same strings that businesses pull to lobby politicians in government for special favors. Cronyism due to political favors is more similar to socialists' heavy government involvement in private affairs than it is to free markets and capitalism. The medicine to reduce cronyism is not more government involvement but rather limiting government intervention as a whole.

The Link Between
Government Spending
and Government Control

Many believe that, as long as our government remains a Republic, we can prevent totalitarianism and horrendous government control. In other words, as long as we have elections, we can avoid the fate of the Soviets and their Commissars. However, there is another way for the government to get absolute control of the private affairs of citizens without an all-powerful tyrant, and that is through taxation and spending.

In an extreme case, consider a democratic country in which 100% of the GDP (or the nation's production) is through government spending. The implications are that 100% of all incomes are taxed and that the amount of goods and services received is purely dictated by the government. This means that everyone works for the government and is provided for by the government, which is no different from a command economy. This means the government has complete control over your savings, spending, and consumption. When a government controls your purse strings, it effectively controls you—what work you do, what you eat, and what kind of house you live in.

As I write this in 2020, total U.S. government spending is approaching 40% of its GDP. This means that *almost half* of our affairs are being dictated by bureaucrats in D.C. This is alarming, considering the fact that, a little more than a hundred years ago, the entire federal government operated on no income tax.[34] The faster the government grows and the faster government spending increases, the less we have for private spending. This means private citizens are making fewer decisions in their lives and have dramatically less economic freedom. Effectively, what this means is that, for every two minutes of your life, one minute is dedicated to what the government tells you to do. Consider how much the government has control over your life when you realize that the government controls the spending of *almost half* of whatever you make.

Spending Your Way Out of Problems, Revisited
Introducing Inflation and the Hidden Tax on Savers

The biggest reason we need to focus on goods produced and not chase dollars is that the failure to understand the difference between the two allows governments to make some ludicrous and overbearing economic decisions. Ultimately, most of these government actions lead to a degradation of freedom, a hidden tax on consumers, and more encroachment on the private lives of citizens, all the while being ineffective in helping the very people it was designed for.

A large body of thought these days involves the idea of government stimulus; spending will benefit everyone. We already addressed that a key issue with spending is that people chase dollars rather than focus on goods and services produced, leading to the misunderstanding that allows people to conclude that as long as we spend more, people are better off.

Let's examine the magic formula again:

Production = Consumption + Capital

First, as we have shown earlier, we know that government spending does not increase the total amount of goods and services produced, since the government doesn't produce anything. Also, we must understand that, when the government spends, the government is spending other people's money. Goods and services that otherwise could be consumed by taxpayers will be consumed by other people as directed by the government.

For example, if the government spends $1,000 of tax money on a park, the people who go walking and playing in the park will consume the government good. If the taxpayers in this case had wanted to spend that $1,000 on strawberries, they would not be able to consume strawberries, and they'd be worse off. This is pretty straightforward, as resources that would have gone into strawberries are re-allocated to a park.

While this is a generally understood concept, the issue becomes murkier when the government deficit spends. To understand this concept better, let's think of Cornville once again. The King of Cornville, in a national emergency—a time of famine—needs to feed 1,000 people. Cornville has produced 1,000 tons of corn this year, and the people of Cornville have saved 200 tons of corn in their personal corn banks and granaries.

The king has subjected 10% of the production of corn to an income tax. This means the king's coffers have 100 tons of corn, but, in order to feed the starving people, he must hand out 200 tons of corn. Very importantly, assuming that, after taxes, the people will consume all their corn this year, if no corn was ever saved in Cornville, this task would be *impossible*. **You can't consume more than you have produced and saved**. However, the king decides to deficit spend (since he knows that Cornville has people willing to lend corn to the king). The king issues corn IOUs. For every ton of corn he borrows, he'll pay back 1.1 tons of corn at the end of the year. To work, however, there must be at least 100 tons of corn in *savings* that the people of Cornville have put away. **Only savers can be lenders**, and they lend to the king. The savers lend 100 tons of corn to the king. Notice, however, that the total amount of corn in this system has not changed. The maximum possible amount of corn that can be consumed today is 1,000 tons—produced this year—plus 200 saved by the people. The total amount of corn consumed today, however, *has* changed. If the king did not borrow 100 tons of corn to give to starving people to eat, the total amount of corn consumed today—assuming that the people would have saved 10% of what they produce before taxes—would have been 1,000 tons minus 100 tons (savings) minus 100 tons (taxes) = 800 tons. But because of the king's deficit spending, the total amount consumed today was the original 800 tons + 200 tons of corn that the king gave out to hungry people. On the surface, it looks as if the country is doing better! After all, the total amount of consumption of corn increased! However, we know that the transferring of corn from savers to the king does not change the total amount of corn produced and saved. We end up paying this back the next year. The 200 tons of corn that the king has spent is gone (consumed by grateful and hungry people). All that the king has done is shifted future consumption (or savings) to today's consumption. The total amount of corn tomorrow will be 100 tons fewer than if he did not tax and distribute the corn.

All of this seems straightforward, should the king give back the 110 tons of corn he promised to lenders. After that, we are back to normal. However, when money is introduced, the picture becomes even murkier. Let's say instead of directly borrowing corn, the king prints corn dollar bills. Let's say that, in Cornville, there are 1,200 corn dollar bills. Because Cornville has a total of 1,200 tons of corn (and that's the only thing it has), the price of corn is 1 corn dollar bill per ton of corn. This has to be the case because if it was worth more than that, then after the 1,200 tons of corn is sold, we still have people who have corn dollar bills willing to exchange the dollars for corn. This means sellers of corn know they can get away with raising prices to get more corn dollar bills. If it were worth less than that, then before 1,200 tons of corn are sold, we have run out of corn dollar bills. The producers of corn know that, in order to sell all the corn they have produced, they must reduce the price of corn relative to corn dollar bills. Notice, the price of corn is *not* something the producers have flexibility over. This relationship between currency and product is very clear in this simple example. In the real world, despite the increased complexity of the relationship between money and goods and services, the general mechanism of how prices change when more currency is printed is the same. If all goods and services are consumed and people still have money to spend, the prices of goods will rise and vice versa.

Let's say the king, instead of borrowing the corn directly, simply prints 100 more corn dollar bills. This seems like a win-win, right? The king can help the starving people, *and* the king doesn't need to borrow from savers, who get to keep their corn. The king buys 100 tons of corn using this newly printed money. Soon, however, the people of Cornville realize that there are now only 1,100 tons of corn (as the king has taken 100 tons and has given it to people to eat), but there are now 1,300 corn dollar bills to go around. The producers realize this, and, to prevent corn from disappearing off the shelves too fast, they have to raise the price of corn in terms of corn dollar bills. This phenomenon is called *inflation*—the prices of goods and services rising.

Inflation is a hidden tax on savers. We've stated numerous times that the people of Cornville cannot possibly be better off, as the total amount of corn in the system did not increase. Where is this hidden tax? The people who have saved corn in the form of corn dollar bills are worse off. With the price increase, they can't buy as much corn as before. They were the ones who were "secretly taxed." Therefore, while, on the surface, it seems like this type of extra spending helps everyone, you can't escape the reality that you can consume only *less* than what you have produced and saved.

In this next part, we'll go into something a little more complex. In our modern economy, when the government deficit spends and increases the money supply, prices do not move very quickly and obviously, compared to the example above. People have now begun to theorize that, as long as prices don't rise, the government can permanently deficit spend to improve the livelihoods of people. After all, inflation is a hidden tax on people, and, if inflation is gone, no one is taxed. From 2008 to 2020, despite record levels of deficit spending, prices of consumer goods, which we use to measure inflation, have barely increased, and the economy has been humming along fantastically.

This conundrum leads us to scratch our heads; it seems as if, by deficit spending, the government is making goods and services out of thin air. After all, we know that the amount of goods and services doesn't increase just because more money was spent. The confusion, I believe, arises because mechanisms for savings have become extremely complex, and the negative effects of deficit spending and increasing the currency or money supply have been masked and delayed.

While inflation of **consumer goods** (such as bread and bikes and cars) has not gone up, inflation in other very important areas has gone up tremendously, just not in ways by which we typically measure it. Most of the extra money supply from deficit spending and stimulus have not gone chasing consumer goods, but chasing investment assets such as stocks, bonds, loans and so on, none of which are measured in the consumer price index, which measures inflation.

We've experienced runaway inflation in investment assets for many years. Between 2009 and 2020, the U.S. stock market has increased roughly 330%, while the nation's productivity grew only 25%[35] in the same time frame. Inflation in asset prices allows the painful effects of deficit spending or printing money to be kicked down the road. All people are happy because they feel they're all getting rich at the same time.

As we showed earlier, printing money is just a means for the government to consume people's savings without an outright confiscation of wealth or an increase in taxes, as you can never consume more than you produce. In the case of the excess money chasing assets, the mechanism that destroys people's savings can happen in two ways:

1. Your current savings will not go as far

Whether you are saving by yourself or through a pension, your current savings will not go as far. If continued deficit spending occurs, real returns on assets will continue to compress to very-low-yielding levels. If you were saving money on your own and you were targeting a certain savings amount at retirement, your current savings will be insufficient. This inflation of asset prices has degraded your future income from your current savings. If you were saving in a pension, your pension will be unable to meet future liabilities with such low yielding asset returns. Currently, pension liabilities are a huge and well-documented black hole that politicians always try to ignore.[36] Either way, you were secretly "taxed" and will experience a worse quality of life in the future when you realize that your savings did not go as far as you anticipated or when your pension is unable pay what it promised.

Stated more simply, if you or your pension is putting away $50 today anticipating to turn those savings into $100 when you retire in 40 years, you will realize that this is an impossible task if the return of all investments is 0% or negative. Therefore, it is clear that the deficit spending of today has secretly taxed your purchasing power in the future.

$ amount needed to be saved today to have $100 in 40 years at different interest rates

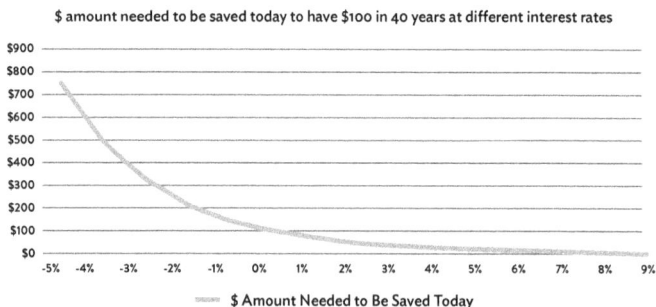

$ Amount Needed to Be Saved Today

2. Your current savings are in risky investments that do not justify the returns

Another mechanism for reality to rear its ugly head when we attempt fiscal stimulus is via realized defaults. Misallocation of investments happens all the time when the government gets involved. As asset prices rise, the only way people can reach their targeted returns and savings is to take more and more risk. The concept of "risk" is typically viewed relative to risk-free rates (government interest rates). However, something in real life also restricts how low returns possibly can be, and those are default rates. If the underlying return of a risky investment is lower than the expected value of the investment, then, in the long run, current savings, which we invest in risky assets that are masked by optimistic current yields and returns, are not positive but actually negative. Therefore, in the long run, current savers are losing money without runaway inflation of consumer goods. They lose their investment when companies default due to the inherently risky nature of businesses and economies. This mechanism is perfect for hiding the disastrous short-term effects of fiscal stimulus because we never know how bad it is until everything explodes via a series of defaults that realizes these probabilistic, expected losses.

Stated more simply, if you invest in a company that promises to pay you 10% every year, but, due to the risks of the economy that can't be controlled, your investment has a probability of default of 20% a year, in the long run, assuming no recoveries on the defaulted investment, you are losing money due to the expected losses you incur. While you may not feel like you are losing money now, when the company goes bankrupt, the losses will come together—all at once.

Do We Need a Reset
of Capital Allocation?

Now that we understand that everything can be divided into spending and savings and that the accumulation of capital is the means to leading a better life, there are certain proponents out there who believe we need to push a reset button on capital allocation.

Society never has been truly free. White westerners imported slaves from Africa in chains, and many white families managed to accumulate large amounts of capital as the beneficiaries of slave labor. Many countries such as Germany and England pillaged China[37] and the British exported tons of opium by force, enriching themselves at the detriment of the average Chinese citizen.

The issue with reallocation of capital is how far back should we go? If you draw the equality line at the 1800s, you can say that white Americans terrorized and took advantage of the Native Americans and black slaves. Go even further, and you'll find that the Native Americans terrorized and conquered each other (think of the Aztecs, the Incas, and the Comanche). Go even further, and you'll find that many of the early slave exporters in Africa were black themselves.[38] Go even further, and you'll find yourself looking at scientific Adam and Eve—*Australopithecus* beings, from which all humans descended—and they certainly had no capital whatsoever. The cutoff for when the "reset" of capital should be is completely arbitrary. Everyone started off from somewhere. The real question we need to ask is that, moving forward in a modern and free society, what's the best way to improve people's everyday lives via the accumulation of capital?

People certainly tried to reallocate capital in many countries and experimented—with disastrous results— with a full redistribution of capital. Communist revolutionaries in China seized land from wealthy landowners and divided it the best they could to poor peasants.[39] Zimbabwe land reforms took primarily from African farmers of European descent (white farmers) and redistributed to the poorer black farmers.[40] There are many reasons why these two great experiments failed, among them are the destruction of incentives to invest, inexperience with capital, and destruction of economies of scale. China entered an era of famine that the world had never seen. It is estimated that more than 45 million people starved to death in China in the 1950s[41] (to put that into context, the number of Jewish people killed in the Holocaust is estimated to be 6 million[42], and the total number of deaths from World War II was 60-110 million[43]). Zimbabwe's economy collapsed and is now used as a case study of the detriments of run-away inflation. The country now primarily subsists on foreign aid.

The last issue is "Who decides?" Notice that, in a free society and free market, no one gets to decide what's fair or what's right. The Free-Market Axioms do not give anyone's interest precedence over another's. In this giant redistribution, who decides who gets what and how far back we go? Why does that person get to decide? Is that person better than us? I don't think there is any good and reasonable answer to these questions.

The Ethical and Practical Issue With Wealth Transfers

The majority of socialist policies rely on wealth transfers or redistribution. The inevitable moral axiom ends up becoming "Might Is Right." If you look at any acts of tyranny today, the first steps involved are the confiscation of wealth, before outright oppression and slaughter. This is because, as we have shown earlier in this book, the moment a person loses his ability to consume what he earns, he forfeits his freedom or life. The protection of property is necessary for the protection of freedom.

Using the new tools we learned in the second half, we know that

Production = Consumption + Savings

Any form of wealth transfer, no matter the cause, is a confiscation of savings for the consumption of another person. Subsidies, food stamps, and affordable housing are, at the end of the day, direct transfers of wealth. There are very few instances in which any kind of confiscation of wealth can be morally sanctioned in a consistent moral system. For any society in which a transfer of wealth is permissible, we are bound to the formula

Production = Consumption + Savings + Loot Stolen From Others – Loot Stolen From You

A society that permits people to steal always takes for granted the left side of the equation, but who in his or her right mind will produce in great quantities, if that person knows that, the next day, it will all be taken away from him or her by bandits, by the taxman, or by the representative doing it for the greater good? Certainly, you can force a person to work—which is called "slavery"—but even a system that relies on slavery will see a rapid stagnation and a fall in production. You can force a person to cut down trees, but you can't force him unleash his innovative and productive powers to invent the saw that will end up benefiting everyone.

As production continues to fall in a society that doesn't respect property rights, we end up with

Production = Consumption + Loot Stolen from Others – Loot Stolen From You

And we are stuck not in not only a cycle of poverty with no savings but also in a cycle of violence.

PART V

THE INTERSECTION OF POLITICS, ECONOMICS, THE LAWS OF NATURE, AND ETHICS

Combining Our Mental Models

Laws of Nature, Moral Systems, and Economic Systems

If food fell from the heavens every day and we could wish anything we wanted into existence, stealing probably wouldn't be a moral issue. Life and the laws of nature dictate what we believe is fair and ethical. If we define fairness and ethics properly, following these guidelines should allow humans to thrive. Deviating from these guidelines should end up in misery and death.

What we determine as a moral system should allow us to determine what an ethical economic system is. In the first section of the book, we built a moral system from scratch, which we called the Free-Market System. We then built an economic model from scratch and showed why we need to use our Free-Market System to best overcome the Laws of Nature.

In the next section of this book, we discuss political systems that best implement our moral and economic systems.

A Political System Should Rely on a Moral System and Not the Other Way Around

One thing that many people misunderstand about America is they believe the great experiment of America was democracy, and these people claim that the Founders' greatest contribution to the world was the idea of democracy. That premise is false. The Greeks and Romans practiced forms of democracy thousands of years ago. The Greeks probably had the purest form of democracy, which allowed for all sorts of atrocities to take place. People could be casually executed as long as enough people voted for it. This included Plato's mentor, Socrates[44]. The early democracies ended up becoming mob rules, where the majority determined what was right and wrong. It also led to bloodshed and tyranny. The Nazi party's rise to power was through a proper democratic election, in which they won a large percentage of the popular vote[45]. The Reign of Terror was committed by the First French Republic—a democracy characterized by mob rule, witch hunts, and daily executions.

Both the Declaration of Independence and the U.S. Constitution do not once mention "democracy." The issue that plagued most of humanity was the fight against **tyranny**. The best way to define "tyranny" is this: A tyrant gets to impose his will upon other people. Tyranny, people found, arises when someone or some group of people have a set of rules or laws that do not apply to the tyrant. In other words, a tyrant can exist only if he is **above the law** in the form of exceptions to the law. Revolutionary Communists would have been less deadly if they themselves were bound by the rules they imposed on others—namely, the rule that forced everyone to contribute his or her personal property to the state. However, the Communists were content with having others contribute to the state and with taking what they needed from the common person. Had they practiced what they preached, the Communists probably would have realized what a horrible system it was and abandoned it. You can have a king or queen who isn't a tyrant if he or she is not above the law. However, the powers that we usually associate with a king or queen typically involve his or her being above the law.

The most famous line in the Declaration of Independence states, "We hold these truths to be self-evident, that all Men are created **equal**, that they are endowed by their Creator with certain unalienable Rights, that among these are Life, Liberty and the pursuit of Happiness . . ." (emphasis added by me)

What could the Founders have meant by "equal"? It certainly wasn't equal in height, or weight, or beauty, or money, but equal in the eyes of the law—but not human laws; it was something higher than that. They are equal such that they cannot be denied their unalienable rights by anyone—no king, no queen, no commissar, and certainly not a democratic majority. Many called this higher law **Natural Law**. I call it an axiomatic system characterized by free markets. No one can be exempt from a system that forbids stealing or murder. That doesn't mean that it's always wrong to kill or confiscate goods; it means that anyone **acting within this framework—trying to kill or steal—is always wrong—no exceptions**.

Under our Free-Market Axiomatic System, there is nothing wrong with any political system, so long as the system does not infringe upon these unalienable rights. In other words, political systems governing how we come up with laws or government are not inherently good or bad. A monarchy that upholds Natural Law or this axiomatic system is moral. A democracy that tramples upon these unalienable rights or flouts the axioms of our system is immoral.

For example, we could have a political system with an absolute and all-powerful monarch who creates laws by himself and can do anything he wants that is moral. This monarch, unlike the tyrants we are used to seeing today, loves the law and hates stealing. He ensures that all his subjects must obey the law, including himself. He punishes thieves by throwing them in prison. He punishes pirates who threaten to extort others by hanging them. One day, he becomes very envious of his neighbor's thoroughbred horse, and, in a moment of weakness, he steals the horse. If the king, on the next day, after calming down, decides to throw himself in prison after being tried as a thief, we can conclude that this political system is a moral one. If the king decides to say to himself, "Dang it, I'm the king, and I get to do what I want," then this political system is an immoral one. This leads to the tyranny we are familiar with. A political system cannot easily be classified as good or bad.

The Founders realized that certain political systems are better at being stable, while others are prone to tyranny. They realized that there must be some sort of restriction in place that prevents governments from easily infringing on people's unalienable rights. In other words, some governments are better than others at trampling upon Natural Law and our axiomatic system. Take the monarchy example above: There really is no way to prevent the king from becoming a tyrant in an absolute monarchy. We just have to trust that he will be a good king. That is not something many would put a lot of faith in.

Therefore, after many years of debate, the Founders set upon a system that can best be described as a **Constitutional Republic**. Notice two things: 1) There is no mention of "democracy," and 2) the word "Constitution" is included.

Regarding point 1), the Founders realized that democracies were just as prone to tyranny as kings. They called it "the tyranny of the masses." After all, does it make any difference if the king steals your horse or that a group of people outnumbering you vote to steal your horse? Simple democracies are perfect conduits for tyranny because their evil deeds are less obvious. Majorities that confiscate wealth and infringe on people's livelihoods and rights can easily claim that it was done for the "greater good," because, by definition, the majority has willed it. I doubt any socialist would claim that whatever the majority votes for is right.

Regarding point 2), the Founders came up with a system of a system of checks and balances that made it extremely difficult for any government organization to become too powerful. They separated what they believed were three key components that, if held together by one entity, would make it very easy for a government to become tyrannical. The three separate branches are the executive (i.e., the president, who **enforces the law**), the legislative (i.e., a congress, which **creates the law**), and the judiciary (i.e., the courts, who **interpret the law**).

Most important, the Founders provided us with the Constitution. The Constitution was the Founders' attempt at codifying an axiomatic system very similar to the one described in this book (although they certainly did not do so using computer-science terms). They believed that the Constitution fully encapsulated Natural Law to create a just and moral system to guide us. The Constitution's primary goal was not to govern the actions of people but to prevent the government from taking certain actions against the people. The Founders intentionally made a very restrictive and weak government.

Natural Law and our Free-Market System say **nothing** about how leaders are chosen, how decisions are made, what national anthem to sing, what religion we should have, and so on. It's up to us to find or choose a system of government and to put it in place to ensure that the axiomatic framework is best preserved.

A big issue with our failed attempts at creating a socialist axiomatic system was that it could not exist by itself. For the system to exist, it required a representative or political system. Therefore, that means that a political system must exist in order for its moral system to exist, which is not self-evident. I doubt any proponent of socialism would say that the only way humans know what is right or wrong is by first establishing a government.

Laws of Nature (and the natural sciences) help us determine what we think is right or wrong (ethics). Ethics allows us to come up with rules and laws (through logic and axioms) that systematically prohibit actions that we deem to be wrong. These rules tell us how to interact with our fellow man in an ethical way to trade and prosper (economics). Finally, we establish a government (politics) to enforce and to ensure that this moral and ethical code is observed by everyone, not the other way around. Neither government nor politics determines what is right or wrong. Ethics does not depend on the way that we organize ourselves politically. Morals, as the Founders believed, are above humans, and no human organization, such as government, can decide what is right or wrong.

PART VI

PRACTICAL ECONOMICS AND ETHICS

No analysis of capitalism would be complete without addressing several weaknesses and issues that free markets cannot solve on their own. We will briefly talk about a few of them to be complete.

Weakness #1
Free Markets Cannot Enforce Laws and Prevent the Breaching of Our Axiomatic System

This is easily the most important reason the preservation and implementation of a Free-Market System requires a government. While it'd be great if everyone agreed to our axiomatic system, many people do not, and they adhere strictly to the policy of "Might Is Right."

The enforcement of laws that embody our moral axioms cannot be done individually. It must be done by a force that no private citizen can overrule. Governments are crucial for protecting individuals' property and to prevent people from coercing others by threat of force. In other words, governments have to have a monopoly on force. After all, the only legal use of force, by definition, is the force of the government. A citizen can't lock someone up (that's called "kidnapping"), but a government can certainly throw a person into prison (that's called "incarcerating").

Courts that arbitrate fairly, under an agreed-upon set of rules, must be provided by our government. Government must provide a police force to enforce the laws and pro-tect citizens from domestic threats, as well as provide for a military that protects its citizens from foreign threats.

Governments have a monopoly on force. This is not a statement to be taken lightly, and, therefore, it must be held to the highest of standards.

Weakness #2
Inability to Provide Public Goods

A key component of a free market is that people must be able to control trades that they enter into. Unfortunately, due to our limited technology and special circumstances, voluntary trade cannot produce certain goods and services, because, at this point, there is no practical way to control who consumes certain goods. We call these goods **public goods**.

Public goods need to meet only one criterion: For practical purposes, when it is impossible to ensure that the person using the good bears its cost, it is a public good. Take, for example, roads. Unless there are tolls on every corner of all the streets, you can't really charge people for using the roads on demand. Similarly, lighthouses and streetlights also meet this standard. You can't stop certain boats from seeing the illumination of your lighthouse or cars who haven't paid your streetlight tax from using the illumination the lights give. Perhaps in the future, as technology advances, you can ensure that only people who buy a digital ticket will be permitted to drive on certain private roads, but, until then, this very limited and strict definition of "public goods" is something that the free market is unable to provide.

Most public goods we see today do not meet this rather strict definition—schools, parks, and bridges, for example. It is easy to see how we can ensure that people who use these services bear the cost. There are many private schools that accept only students who enroll and pay for classes. Disneyland is a massive park that is run extremely well and grants admission to ticket purchasers. Bridges need only a toll station on either end to ensure that those who use the bridge will pay.

Private goods that are provided publicly create inefficiency, as they are subtle forms of wealth transfers. For example, a park that is built with tax money provides a free park for all the people to use. However, is it truly free? Of course not. Depending on the tax scheme, everybody bears some cost of the park. Unless this tax burden for the park matches exactly how much someone is willing to pay to go to the park, then by definition, a provision of this "public" good destroys value. A private institution that bears the cost of running the park will be incentivized to run it as efficiently as possible.

Weakness #3
Negative and Positive Externalities

In the first section of the book, we focused on the definition of "Harm." We talked about how harm needed to be an action that was direct; otherwise, it opens a whole new can of worms. However, there are actions taken in which other people will bear costs involuntarily. We call these *negative externalities*. The most common negative externality is pollution. If I pour toxic waste into my backyard and poison the soil under the neighborhood, everyone living in that area will get sick. My actions have costs to others that I am not bearing.

Negative externalities are immoral, according to even our strict definition of "Harm." This is because the most common negative externalities that we are aware of—such as pollution, congestion, and loud noises—do measurably make someone else worse off. Negative externalities needn't necessarily be removed entirely. We just need to ensure that the cost of the person producing the negative externality is borne by him or her.

The tricky thing with negative externalities is that they are extremely hard to measure and are sometimes not obvious. In a free market, we have numerous voluntary transactions that people undertake to determine the true cost of certain goods and services. In the case of determining the value of the negative externality, we cannot rely on the free market to determine the cost. We can't give a survey out to people that says, "How much would you pay not to have pollution and smoke drifting around in your neighborhood?" Everyone would just answer "$1 billion," since they don't want pollution in their backyards. Another problem is that, in many instances, negative externalities are hard to prove. Before we could readily regulate areas where people are allowed to smoke, we first needed to figure out that smoking and secondhand smoke can kill you, which took some time.

However, under careful definitions of what constitutes a negative externality (an action taken by someone that causes a concrete and measurable negative effect on someone else), the government can use effective tools such as taxes (carefully and best measured to one's ability) to ensure that producers of negative externalities bear the cost.

The argument of negative externalities is usually abused by a government to regulate areas that they otherwise would not be able to. Arguments that rely on immeasurable and dodgy science to estimate potential (and sometimes false) second-, third-, and fourth-order effects can show that practically every action taken by anybody is a negative externality, which many politicians use to justify any sort of government intervention in the daily lives of people. That would effectively undermine all our axioms and our system of freedom. Therefore, when determining negative externalities, people should err on the side of no intervention, unless there is overwhelming evidence.

Similarly (but more rarely), the free market does not do a good job of producing goods and services that generate a benefit that someone is not paying for. For example, vaccines benefit not only the person getting the shot but also all the people who interact with this person, as it drastically reduces the chance of spreading such disease. Usually the tool at the government's disposal is to subsidize the production of these goods. Like negative externalities, many times governments lean on this argument to try to subsidize any people or industries as political favors. Therefore, unless there is overwhelming evidence of a measurable positive externality of producing certain goods and services, people should err on the side of no intervention.

Weakness #4
Monopolies

Throughout the examples above, a lot of the efficiencies of a free market depend on the fact that firms are in a competitive environment, which, in most free markets and for most goods and services, is true.

However, there are examples of firms becoming effective monopolies that can theoretically raise their prices well above their economic costs for high levels of profit, to the detriment of consumers. While theoretically true, we've yet to see the large negative effects of a modern monopoly (absent cronyism and lobbying). The amount of goods and services produced by firms that many people believe are monopolies, such as Google, Facebook, and Microsoft, has been tremendous for the entire world. We won't spend too much time on monopolies, as they are few and far between. The numbers on the effects of monopolies certainly is not a settled science and are very difficult to measure. Even defining a monopoly is extremely hard to do consistently. Before proposing radical legislation or government intervention on monopolies, we need to determine 1) Whether a true monopoly in a free market can possibly exist (outside of a natural monopoly), 2) whether any true monopoly currently exists, and 3) whether true monopolies actually harm their customers in a measurable way.

PRACTICAL ETHICS AND ECONOMICS

Practically speaking, we want to live in a moral society and solve all the problems we face. In an ideal world, all goods and services produced should be traded through voluntary agreements. An implication of our Free-Market Axiomatic System is that all goods and services that *can* be produced by an individual *should* be produced by an individual. Milton Friedman said, "History only suggests that capitalism is a necessary condition for political freedom. Clearly, it is not a sufficient condition[46]." To truly be free, people must be economically free. If a government or separate entity controls what you eat, when you eat it, and where you eat it, it controls you without the threat of a gun. It is imperative that, to preserve our liberty, we preserve our ability to conduct our businesses and interactions freely in society without government involvement or coercion.

PART VII

FINAL THOUGHTS

We now have a very simple but robust model of how the world works from an ethical, economic, and political perspective. Where does this leave us, and what should be the most-important takeaways from what you've read?

First, I hope that it allows you to appreciate how far we've come as a species. Some examples here should give you a sense of proportion about where we are. Your immediate reaction when you encounter a problem is not to propose a revolution and a total destruction of the current world order. Many people have tried before to destroy free markets, private ownership, and capitalism to promote equality with disastrous results. Millions have died, and many more have been enslaved. Look at the mass graves in Cambodia and the unmarked graves in Ukraine, and understand that all of that was done in the name of equality, fairness, and the good of the people. Due to their fundamental misunderstanding of basic economics and ethics, many people with good intentions supported tyrannical regimes and allowed such atrocities to happen. I hope this book also gives you a glimpse of how great an experiment the creation of the United States was. In terms of both ethics and the expansion of rights of the common person by the limiting of government powers, there truly is no country like America, and I don't know if there ever will be another.

Second, I hope it gives you a model to lean on for critical thinking in the future. As opposed to the usual logical fallacies strewn around in the world of politics today, it is up to us to think of things rationally, clearly, and, most importantly (I can't emphasize this enough), **consistently**. While there is compromise in arbitrating disputes, there is no compromise in ethics. Stealing cannot be right for some while illegal for others. Laws can change, but they cannot be changed on a whim, like so many are prone to today. Otherwise, ethics just comes down to whose whim is more powerful, which is no different than fascism. Ethical consistency is not a luxury. The framework for ethics and thinking about ethics needs to remain as solid as ever in even the direst of emergencies and circumstances. There's a reason that no politician lets a crisis go to waste to expand his or her political power.

Third, I hope that you will learn that simplification and stepping back allows you to glean many useful things about the world. Many times, we get lost in the complexity of the modern economy, and we start believing a politician's promise that, if elected, he or she can magically, through the waving of a bureaucrat's stamp, turn one strawberry into two and that the only cost will be your freedom. Be wary of those who promise all sorts of goods and benefits without ever mentioning anything about costs. *There ain't no such thing as a free lunch.*

Too often people want their cake and eat it, too. Those who argue the most fervently against capitalism write their anti-free-market views on laptops produced and invented by capitalists with money they earned by being a capitalist trading with another capitalist. However, taking a further step back, the biggest difference between an advocate of free markets and its opponents comes down to one key word: choice.

A free person doesn't care if a socialist wants to live in a socialist utopia, but socialists will always force free people to be part of their socialist utopia. Watch how people vote with their feet. People's feet speak the loudest when they move from one place to another in search of happiness and fulfillment. Are certain governments forcing people to stay in their utopian country, or are they trying their best to prevent too many people from coming into their utopian country? Can you force people to stay and do what you want in your utopia for their own good?

For a person who believes in freedom and the Free-Market Axiomatic System, the questions above are easy to answer. Let people do what they want, as long as they don't hurt others. For socialists, it's an extremely complex answer. At the end of the day, watch who is advocating a policy that tells people what to do by force via the government. Think critically about the world, and understand how it works. Lastly, cherish your liberties, and never take them for granted.

Sources

1. Booth, Alan D. 1979. "The Schooling of Slaves in First-Century Rome." *Transactions of the American Philological Association* 109:11–1.
2. H. V. Harris, *Ancient Literacy* (Harvard University Press, 1989) 328.
3. Maybury, R. (2015). "Tanstaafl, the Romans, and Us," In *Whatever Happened to Penny Candy?* (p. 23). Placerville, CA: Bluestocking Press.
4. Maybury, R. J. (2004). "Enforcement of Early Common Law," in *Whatever Happened to Justice?* (pp. 41-44). Placerville, CA: Bluestocking Press.
5. GDP per capita (current US $). (n.d.). Retrieved April 19, 2021, from https://data.worldbank.org/indicator/NY.GDP.PCAP.CD
6. GDP, PPP (current international $). (2019). Retrieved October 24, 2020, from https://data.worldbank.org/indicator/NY.GDP.MKTP.PP.CD
7. "Visualizing Income Percentiles in the United States." (2019, December 4). Retrieved October 24, 2020, from https://fourpillarfreedom.com/visualizing-income-percentiles-in-the-united-states/
8. "United States Economics." (2019). Retrieved October 24, 2020, from https://datacommons.org/place/country/USA?topic=Economics

9. HHS POVERTY GUIDELINES FOR 2020. (2020, March 5). Retrieved October 24, 2020, from https://aspe.hhs.gov/poverty-guidelines

10. Joszt, L. (2019, October 25). "Medicare Patients With Blood Cancer Face High Costs That May Impact Treatment." Retrieved August 15, 2020, from https://www.ajmc.com/focus-of-the-week/medicare-patients-with-blood-cancer-face-high-costs-that-may-impact-treatment

11. Aggregate Total Hospital Margins and Operating Margins. (2016). Retrieved April 18, 2021, from https://www.aha.org/system/files/2018-05/2018-chartbook-table-4-1.pdf

12. Cancer Statistics. (n.d.). Retrieved August 15, 2020, from https://www.cancer.gov/about-cancer/understanding/statistics

13. "Universal Declaration of Human Rights." (n.d.). Retrieved October 24, 2020, from https://www.un.org/en/universal-declaration-human-rights/

14. "Free College, Cancel Debt." (n.d.). Retrieved October 24, 2020, from https://berniesanders.com/issues/free-college-cancel-debt/

15. Friedman, M. (n.d.). "The Role of Government in a Free Society." Retrieved August 15, 2020, from https://miltonfriedman.hoover.org/friedman_images/Collections/2016c21/1978TheRoleofGovernment.pdf

16. Apostolides, A., Broadberry, S., Campbell, B., Overton, M., & Leeuwen, B. V. (2008, November 26). "English Gross Domestic Product, 1300-1700: Some Preliminary Estimates." Retrieved August 15, 2020, from https://warwick.ac.uk/fac/soc/economics/staff/sbroadberry/wp/pre1700v2.pdf

17. Friesen, S., & Scheidel, W. (2008, November 14). The Size of the Economy and the Distribution of Income in the Roman Empire. Retrieved November 11, 2020, from https://papers.ssrn.com/sol3/papers.cfm?abstract_id=1299313

18. Watkins, D., & Brook, Y. (2016). "The Conditions of Progress," in *Equal Is Unfair: America's Misguided Fight Against Income Inequality* (p. 86). New York: St. Martin's Press.

19. Smith, N. (2018, January 18). "Yup, Rent Control Does More Harm Than Good." Retrieved September 22, 2020, from https://www.bloomberg.com/opinion/articles/2018-01-18/yup-rent-control-does-more-harm-than-good

20. China & Asia Cultural Travel. (n.d.). Retrieved November 11, 2020, from https://www.asiaculturaltravel.co.uk/the-western-jin-dynasty/

21. Driving for Uber Eats: What Is it Like Delivering Food for Uber? (2020, October 06). Retrieved November 11, 2020, from https://www.ridesharingdriver.com/driving-for-ubereats-what-its-like-delivering-food-for-uber/

22. "5 Reasons to Love *Mad Men's* New Star: The IBM 360." (2015, June 11). Retrieved August 15, 2020, from https://www.nbcnews.com/tech/gadgets/5-reasons-love-mad-mens-new-star-ibm-360-n101716

23. Online Food Delivery—United States: Statista Market Forecast. (n.d.). Retrieved November 11, 2020, from https://www.statista.com/outlook/374/109/online-food-delivery/united-states

24. Roser, M. (n.d.). "The short history of global living conditions and why it matters that we know it." Retrieved October 24, 2020, from https://ourworldindata.org/a-history-of-global-living-conditions-in-5-charts

25. Watkins, D., & Brook, Y. (2016). "The Conditions of Progress," in *Equal Is Unfair: America's Misguided Fight Against Income Inequality* (p. 98). New York: St. Martin's Press.

26. Tarver, E. (2020, August 28). "Where Does Warren Buffett Keep His Money?" Retrieved October 24, 2020, from https://www.investopedia.com/articles/investing/011216/where-does-warren-buffett-keep-his-money.asp

27. *Investopedia*. (2020, August 28). Warren Buffett's Annual Salary at Berkshire Hathaway. Retrieved October 24, 2020, from https://www.investopedia.com/ask/answers/020915/what-warren-buffetts-annual-salary-berkshire-hathaway.asp

28. Son, H. (2020, March 21). "Goldman Sachs CEO David Solomon Gets a 20% Raise to $27.5 Million for His work in 2019." Retrieved October 24, 2020, from https://www.cnbc.com/2020/03/20/goldman-sachs-ceo-david-solomon-gets-a-20percent-raise-to-27point5-million-for-his-work-in-2019.html

29. Bhuva, R. (2018, February 26). Warren Buffett's report card. Retrieved November 11, 2020, from https://www.fortuneindia.com/investing/warren-buffetts-report-card/101623

30. Radford-Wattley, A. (2020, June 8). How much is Kim Jong Un worth? Retrieved November 11, 2020, from https://www.foxbusiness.com/lifestyle/how-much-is-kim-jong-un-worth

31. Friedman, M. (n.d.). Friedman on Capitalism and Freedom. Retrieved November 11, 2020, from https://oll.libertyfund.org/pages/friedman-on-capitalism-and-freedom

32. National Association of Insurance Commissioners. (2019). "U.S. Health Insurance Industry 2018 Annual Results." Retrieved August 15, 2020, from https://naic.org/

documents/topic_insurance_industry_snapshots_2018_
health_ins_ind_report.pdf

33. Biery, M. E. (2018, January 26). "Restaurants' Margins Are
Fatter, but Competition Is Fierce." Retrieved August 15, 2020,
from https://www.forbes.com/sites/sageworks/2018/01/26/
restaurants-margins-are-fatter-but-competition-is-fierce/

34. 16th Amendment to the U.S. Constitution: Federal Income
Tax (1913). (n.d.). Retrieved November 11, 2020, from
https://www.ourdocuments.gov/doc.php?flash=false

35. Gross Domestic Product. (2021, March 25). Retrieved
April 19, 2021, from https://fred.stlouisfed.org/series/GDP

36. Krouse, S. (2018, July 30). The pension hole for U.S. cities
and states is the size of Germany's economy. Retrieved
February 06, 2021, from https://www.wsj.com/articles/
the-pension-hole-for-u-s-cities-and-states-is-the-size-of-
japans-economy-1532972501

37. "Troops of the Eight-Nation Alliance, 1900." (2017, October
14). Retrieved August 15, 2020, from https://rarehistorical-
photos.com/troops-eight-nation-alliance-1900/

38. Nwaubani, A. T. (2019, September 20). "When the
Slave Traders Were African." Retrieved August 15,
2020, from https://www.wsj.com/articles/when-the-slave
-traders-were-african-11568991595

39. "1950: The Land Reform." (2009, September 15). Retrieved
August 15, 2020, from http://www.china.org.cn/features/
60years/2009-09/15/content_18530605.htm

40. Hammond, A. (2018, September 04). "Why Mugabe's
Land Reforms Were so Disastrous." Retrieved August 15,
2020, from https://www.cato.org/publications/commentary/
why-mugabes-land-reforms-were-so-disastrous

41. Somin, I. (2016, August 03). "Remembering the Biggest Mass Murder in the History of the World." Retrieved August 15, 2020, from https://www.washington-post.com/news/volokh-conspiracy/wp/2016/08/03/giving-historys-greatest-mass-murderer-his-due/

42. "Documenting Numbers of Victims of the Holocaust and Nazi Persecution." (n.d.). Retrieved October 24, 2020, from https://encyclopedia.ushmm.org/content/en/article/documenting-numbers-of-victims-of-the-holocaust-and-nazi-persecution

43. "Research Starters: Worldwide Deaths in World War II: The National WWII Museum": New Orleans. (n.d.). Retrieved October 24, 2020, from https://www.nationalww2museum.org/students-teachers/student-resources/research-starters/research-starters-worldwide-deaths-world-war

44. Torcello, L., Associate Professor of Philosophy. (2020, August 12). "Why Tyranny Could Be the Inevitable Outcome of Democracy." Retrieved August 15, 2020, from https://theconversation.com/why-tyranny-could-be-the-inevitable-outcome-of-democracy-126158

45. "How Did the Nazis Consolidate Their Power?" (n.d.). Retrieved October 24, 2020, from https://www.theholocaustexplained.org/the-nazi-rise-to-power/how-did-the-nazi-gain-power/1933-elections/

About the Author

Benjamin Chang was born and raised on the outskirts of Beijing, China. By the time he finished high school, he had witnessed firsthand the stunning transformation of his sleepy suburb from acres of quiet farmland to sprawling malls and shopping centers. Since then, he's had a passion for economics. Chang graduated with honors form Carnegie Mellon University with a double major in finance and computer science. His particular interests include logic, proofs, investing, and cartoons. If he isn't jamming on the guitar to his favorite Elvis song, you can almost always find him on a tennis court trying desperately to improve his inconsistent backhand.

www.ingramcontent.com/pod-product-compliance
Lightning Source LLC
Chambersburg PA
CBHW071210210326
41597CB00016B/1756